20 (*Surprisingly Simple*)

RULES *and* TOOLS *for a* GREAT FAMILY

Tyndale House Publishers, Inc., Carol Stream, Illinois

FOCUS ON THE FAMILY
RESOURCES

Surprisingly Simple

20 RULES
and TOOLS
for a GREAT
FAMILY

DR. STEVE STEPHENS

Visit Tyndale's exciting Web site at www.tyndale.com

TYNDALE and Tyndale's quill logo are registered trademarks of Tyndale House Publishers, Inc.

20 (Surprisingly Simple) Rules and Tools for a Great Family

Copyright © 2006 by Steve Stephens. All rights reserved.

Cover photo copyright © by Alloy Photography/Veer. All rights reserved.

Stephens family photo copyright © by Yuen Lui Studios, Inc. All rights reserved.

Designed by Jessie McGrath

Scripture quotations are taken from the *Holy Bible*, New International Version®. NIV®. Copyright © 1973, 1978, 1984 by International Bible Society. Used by permission of Zondervan. All rights reserved.

Library of Congress Cataloging-in-Publication Data

Stephens, Steve
  20 (surprisingly simple) rules and tools for a great family / Steve Stephens.
    p. cm.
  Includes bibliographical references and index.
  ISBN-13: 978-1-4143-0599-8 (sc : alk. paper)
  ISBN-10: 1-4143-0599-0 (sc : alk.paper)
  1. Family—Religious aspects—Christianity.   2. Parenting—Religious aspects—Christianity. I. Title.
  BT707.7.S74 2006
  248.8'45—dc22
                                                     2006006536

Printed in the United States of America

12 11 10 09 08 07 06
7   6   5   4   3   2   1

CONTENTS

Getting Started 1

Wrapping Up 199

GETTING STARTED

"IT'S TIME."

"Right now?" I asked, as the adrenaline pumped through my body and I jumped out of bed. Even though the digital alarm clock read 3:45, I was wide awake.

"I think so," Tami said.

Moments later we were in the car, racing toward the hospital. We were both so excited about being first-time parents, but I also felt some nervousness. As we drove into the hospital's parking lot, I took Tami's hand and said, "Our life will never be the same."

At the time I had no idea how true those words would be. When a couple welcomes their first child into the world, everything is turned upside down. Suddenly you're a family. The rules of life change. You have pressures, feelings, and responsibilities that can seem overwhelming. You now must deal with the care and growth of a little human being. Many new parents aren't sure what to do. Some had good examples of parenting; some didn't.

If only there were a manual that taught us step-by-step how to create a perfect family. But unfortunately such a guide doesn't exist. In fact, perfect families don't exist. We all have our struggles and challenges.

Every family—a combination of unique backgrounds and unique personalities—faces unique situations. While there might not be any guaranteed formula to building a great family, there are a number of tried-and-true rules that will help you move in the right direction.

Most of us aren't excited about rules. They make life feel too rigid and structured. Rules also cause us to feel guilty if we don't follow them perfectly. But whether we want to admit it or not, rules also offer a certain sense of security. They provide order and protect us from chaos.

Every family has its own specific rules. Rules such as:

- Don't hit.

- Do your chores.

- Flush.

- Brush your teeth.

- Put things where they belong.

That's just the way things work. If you follow the rules, family life runs more smoothly. If you break the rules, daily life gets a little bumpy.

Then there are the general rules. They involve basic principles, and they are even more important than the specific rules. As you turn the pages of this book, you'll find twenty practical rules based on these principles. I have discovered these rules in my work with hundreds of families over the past twenty-five years as a psychologist specializing in marriage and family issues. The rules are surprisingly simple, and when applied consistently, they can help keep us on track as a family.

These rules also come from personal life experience. Tami and I have been married twenty-two years, and we have three children. We have had wonderful times together, and we have had rough times. Sometimes my family makes me laugh, and sometimes they drive me nuts. Sometimes they make me so frustrated I want to move to Australia. And I suppose (if I'm totally honest) there are days I frustrate them so much that they want me to move to Australia. But we all love each other, even if we don't feel it every moment of every day.

Family life can be hard. I've learned the importance of these rules because I've seen what happens when they're broken. I'm still learning (just ask Tami), but I'm better now than I was a year or two ago. And hopefully, I'll be even better a year or two from now.

Rules from professional and personal experience are important, but they aren't the most crucial thing. Everything I discover as a psychologist and family counselor I run through the grid of the Holy Bible. God's Word is my foundation; with it as my frame of reference, I know I will not stray far from the truth. And the truth is what ultimately matters!

Each chapter in this book will explain one of the rules and show why it's important. After each rule, you'll find three tools. I've included these tools because, while information might make interesting reading, it's the application of the information that makes a great family. These tools will help you apply the rules in a way that is simple but profound. The tools include:

> **Prayer**: a way to seek God's help in getting you on track and keeping you there

Passage: a quotation from the Bible that will give you God's perspective

Practice: a few assignments to help you insert the rules into the ups and downs of everyday life

By now you're probably ready to jump into the rules. So read on and give these twenty rules a try. Talk about them as a family. Modify them to fit your particular situation. Then put them into practice. You'll be amazed as you see your family:

grow closer

grow happier

grow more positive

grow more healthy

Family life will never be perfect, but it can definitely get better.

RULE ❶
PLAN AHEAD

"WHAT'S THE PLAN, Dad?"

"What would you guys like to do?" I asked my two boys.

"I'd like to get an ice cream cone," said Dusty.

"And I'd like to ride bikes," said Dylan.

"Let's do both," I said. "First, we'll eat supper, then let's ride our bikes down to Baskin-Robbins. After that we can ride to Grandma and Grandpa's to see their brand-new kittens."

And that is exactly what we did.

Life gets so busy and hectic that often my good intentions don't turn into reality. I often think of all the things I really wanted to do but somehow never did. Then I'm left with regrets. So what is the key? It's simple: *Plan ahead*. Here are five of the lessons I've learned:

   ① If I don't plan it, it doesn't happen.

   ② If I don't schedule it, other things squeeze it out.

   ③ If I don't write it down, I forget it.

   ④ If I don't discuss it, other people don't know about it.

   ⑤ I'm not specific, the details don't fit together.

The best things in life begin with some sort of plan. Architects plan buildings. Cooks plan meals. Teachers plan lessons. Every once in a while an accident creates something great, but usually accidents just create a mess. The more important something is, the more intentional I want to be about it. H. Ross Perot said: "Anything that is really worthwhile must be kept on the cutting edge and constantly fought for." A great family is one of the most worthwhile things in the world. It's something we should all fight for. I want my family to be healthy and happy, strong and successful. I want us to reach out to others and reach up to God.

I won't be satisfied with an average family; I want a *great* family. It doesn't take a lot of work to be above average, but it does require a plan. Great families don't just happen. We live in a culture where there are a lot of factors to distract us from being the sort of family we want to be. We all struggle with issues such as:

- overscheduling

- materialism

- exhaustion

- negative influences

Trying to raise a great family is like fighting a never-ending battle. Dr. David Clark writes, "When you're in a war, you need a battle plan. You won't win the war without one." Yet most families don't have a plan. Maybe that is why so many feel as if they are losing the war.

But don't give up.

There is hope.

We just need to set up a plan and follow through. Here are three questions to help you get your plan started.

WHAT PARENTING STYLE DO YOU WANT TO USE?

We each learn how to run a family by watching our parents. Some of us had parents who knew how to build great families. Yet many had parents who didn't have a clue. Most parents do the best they can, given their circumstances. But because of poor training, alcoholism, financial difficulties, anger, divorce, abuse, demanding jobs, medical conditions, stress, or a host of other challenges, your parents might not have parented to the best of their abilities. In fact, up to this point, you might not have parented to the best of your abilities.

But the past is the past.

Right now is a great time for a fresh start. Let go of your past mistakes and excuses. You can begin to improve your own parenting style by avoiding five popular traps. At various times each of us has fallen into at least one of these traps. Don't beat yourself up; just be aware of them so that you can make a plan to avoid them in the future.

The trap of overprotection: *Overprotective* parents are worried that something bad will happen to their children if they give them too much freedom. They want their children to be safe and are willing to do whatever it takes to protect them. The message of this parenting style is, "Always be careful; it's a dangerous world out there." But often the fear of these parents increases their children's fear, or it smothers their children and causes them to want to escape.

The trap of permissiveness: *Permissive* parents are way too easy, often caving in to the pressures and wishes of their children. Sometimes they don't set clear limits; sometimes they just have trouble enforcing the limits. They love their children and believe that being a friend, rather than a parent, will build a closer relationship. The message of this parenting style is, "Whatever you want, you can have." The problem here is twofold. Children frequently don't know what's best for them, and they are set up with unrealistic expectations for the future if they get whatever they want now.

The trap of controlling: *Controlling* parents want to control everything: their children's time, friends, hobbies, opinions, clothing styles. They are always right, and they resent it when anyone challenges them. They are stubborn, strong willed, and heavy handed. This parent requires immediate obedience without question or clarification. The message of this parenting style is, "Do it my way, and do it immediately—or else." Controlling parents tend to squelch their child's spirit or foster a spirit of rebellion.

The trap of criticism: *Critical* parents expect perfection. Nothing their children do is ever good enough. These parents tend to be impatient, negative, and critical. They push their children, evaluating everything they do. They set impossibly high standards, constantly focusing on what is wrong and what needs to be improved. The message of this parenting style is, "If you can't do it right, you'd better keep trying until you can." Their children either push themselves to be perfect and are never satisfied with themselves, or they give up, realizing they can't meet their parents' standards.

The trap of distance: *Disconnected* parents live in the same house, but each person does his or her own thing. In today's fast-paced world, it is easy for parents to become disconnected. They are so involved in their own activities that they don't take the extra time to truly connect with their children. They only have superficial involvement. The message of this parenting style is, "We're so busy that you'll have to meet your own needs." These children might feel lonely, isolated, rejected, or unimportant. They also might crave attention so much that as they get older, they find themselves in serious romantic relationships before they are ready.

So now that we've seen how not to parent, how do we know what is a healthy style? I believe that there's some truth to be found in each of these styles. By taking these truths and adding a good measure of love, you can create a solid parenting style to build and develop your family.

- Be cautious, not *overprotective*.

- Be generous, not *permissive*.

- Be firm, not *controlling*.

- Be encouraging, not *critical*.

- Be involved, not *distant*.

A healthy parenting style rarely happens by itself. It requires positive choices, and these choices are much easier if we plan ahead.

WHAT VALUES DO YOU WANT TO TEACH?

Great intentions don't turn into reality without a plan. Good behavior doesn't happen unless it's taught, modeled, and encouraged. In our family, certain values are important to us. I've thought about them, I've written them down, and I've talked to my children about them. When Moses was sharing God's values with his people he said, "Do not forget the things your eyes have seen or let them slip from your heart as long as you live. Teach them to your children and to their children after them, . . . talking about them when you sit at home and when you walk along the road, when you lie down and when you get up" (Deuteronomy 4:9; 11:19). So let me share twelve core values we've talked about in my family:

Faith: Looking to and leaning on God while doing what he wants us to do.

Compassion: Showing love, care, and consideration for those in need.

Responsibility: Working hard to do what needs to be done, and doing it well.

Integrity: Being a person of honesty who does what is good and right, regardless of the cost.

Respect: Having proper regard for people, places, and things.

Communication: Sharing your thoughts and emotions in ways that are clear and caring.

Growth: Learning to be a better person intellectually, emotionally, physically, socially, and spiritually.

Kindness: Making sure our words, actions, and thoughts toward others are positive.

Patience: Letting God work according to his timetable.

Togetherness: Spending time talking, laughing, listening, working, and playing, side by side.

Courage: Standing up for what is right, and not allowing fear to control us.

Generosity: Giving sacrificially to God, family, friends, and others.

These twelve values provide a powerful, positive direction for my family. As I follow them and pass them on to my children, I am building a great family. There aren't many places where healthy values are taught, and I want my family to be one of those places. So I must plan ahead to determine what I am going to teach. But that is the easy part; the hard part is actually doing it.

WHAT DREAMS DO YOU WANT TO PURSUE?

I have great dreams for my marriage, for my children, and for my family. I actually have hundreds of dreams. I want my relationship with Tami to improve every year. I want my children to love others and love God. I want my family to enjoy spending time together. I come from a family of six children, and we still get together often—for birthdays, holidays, and many other occasions. Several years ago, four of us joined my parents for a trip to Mexico. A month ago some of us helped my youngest brother move. We like to hang out, play basketball, listen to music, and go to movies. When my children get older, I hope they will still want to spend time with Tami and me. Yet for this to happen, we need to build a sense of family now.

Every family needs to talk about its dreams. Without dreams, it's easy to lose your sense of excitement and cohesiveness. Jim Morris said in the movie *The Rookie,* "If you don't have dreams, you don't have anything." He has a point, but we need to take that one step further. Dreams won't take you anywhere unless you have a plan to turn them into reality. The first step is to put your dreams in writing. You might even have each member of your family do the same. Our family's dreams are varied but achievable. Brittany and Dylan want to take a family cruise in the Caribbean. Dusty would like us to stay home and play more board games. Tami would like our family to read more. And I want us to go on a mission trip to help families in third world countries. With a little planning, each of these dreams can happen. In fact, I've noticed that Tami has been on the Internet lately looking up information about cruises. And just last week I saw all three children reading. With patience and planning, dreams do come true.

PLAN TIME TO PLAN

Thursday nights, when all the children are tucked cozily in their beds, Tami and I talk. We look at our calendars and discuss what is scheduled for the weekend. We also talk about what we'd like to see happen over the next few days. Then we plan ahead. We figure out what we are going to do, when we are going to do it, and how it will get done. This weekly planning time keeps us on track and makes sure good things get done. With good planning, you, too, will be able to master the principles outlined in the following chapters!

The reality is that great families plan ahead.

TODAY'S TOOLS

Prayer

Dear God,

Thank you for giving me the gift of a family. Thank you so much for my children—even when they wear me out or make me worry or drive me crazy.

Help me to celebrate all I do well as a parent and admit all those areas where I struggle.

Help me to be a better parent. Help me to let go of all my past frustrations and failures. Help me to be the type of parent you want me to be.

Forgive me for all the times I have been overprotective, too permissive, controlling, critical, or distant. Show me how to love my children like you love me.

Direct my ways and teach me how to plan ahead.

Let today be the beginning of a new and exciting day when I become a better parent and my children draw closer together as we, with your help, build a great family.

Amen.

Passage

Sons are a heritage from the LORD, children a reward from him.
Psalm 127:3

Practice

① Make a list of all the things that keep you from planning ahead.

② Consider which of the five popular traps of parenting—being over-protective, permissive, controlling, critical, or distant—you fall into most often.

③ Think through the three most important values you want to build into your children. Discuss with other parents what they think the three most important values are.

④ Talk to your kids about what dreams they would like to see come true in the next year and the next five years.

RULE ❷
ADMIT YOUR MISTAKES

"WHAT'S YOUR MOST important tool?"

The carpenter looked at the little boy and smiled. "My nail puller."

"Why a nail puller?"

"Because sometimes I make a mistake, and I have to fix it. The best way to do that is to pull the nail and try again."

All parents make their share of mistakes. When this happens, we can ignore it and pretend it never happened. Unfortunately this usually leaves you with a bent nail or a crooked board—something that's not quite right. Or you can swallow your pride and pull some nails. I hate pulling nails, but that's just part of life.

No one likes to face his or her mistakes. Yet as parents, this is a great opportunity to improve our skills and strengthen our families. Every family has its bent nails, and if we don't make the proper repairs we can get into trouble. By admitting our mistakes, we build closer relationships, model honesty, and improve our chances of building a great family.

ADMIT IT

Parenting is not easy. You want to make the right decisions, but sometimes it's difficult to know what to do. No matter who you are, I guarantee you'll never be the perfect parent. You blow it and I blow it; that's life. When my son Dusty was nine, I asked him if he ever lied. Without hesitation he looked me in the eye and said, "Yes, because 'all have sinned and fall short of the glory of God'" (Romans 3:23). Then he thought for a moment and said, "Dad, do you know why that's such a good verse?" I shook my head. "It's because you can use it almost every day." Dusty was right: We all fail every day.

Admitting that you can't and won't be perfect takes a lot of pressure off. Give yourself permission to make mistakes. I have found that the harder I try to be perfect, the more mistakes I make. So I give myself a 20 percent "margin of error." That means it's okay if what I'm doing isn't perfect. I still try to do my best, I just don't obsess or worry about it.

I've spoken to thousands of parents. I have found that most of them truly love their children and do the best they can. Yet I've also found that even well-intentioned parents make a lot of mistakes. Some of the most common mistakes include being:

- too harsh

- too easy

- too busy

- too impatient

- too distracted

- too selfish

- too reactive

- too angry

- too stressed

- too negative

- too fearful

- too stubborn

If you are like most parents, you can probably think of times you have made at least some of these mistakes. We all fail at times, but this doesn't mean we are bad parents. The first step in getting back on track is to admit our mistakes.

Admitting your failures and weaknesses is sometimes harder than it should be. Too many parents want to maintain an image that they are always right and always in control. But this just isn't true. So don't let your pride get in the way. Just say it: "I was wrong," "You were right," "I sure blew that," or "I don't know what I was thinking." It's healthy to admit you were wrong. It models honesty, humility, and vulnerability to your children—three virtues that will help them through a lifetime of challenges.

APOLOGIZE FOR IT

Once you've admitted that you are human, you may need to apologize for your attitude, words, or actions. Yet when things go wrong, it's easy to withdraw or get angry. Instead of taking responsibility, we try to shift the blame. But when we admit our mistakes and apologize, our children learn the importance of personal accountability. Just say, "I'm so sorry

I messed up." It's amazing how forgiving children are—if their parents simply apologize.

When Dylan was seven, he loved soccer. One beautiful September day I went out to play soccer with my son. We kicked the ball and played one-on-one and laughed together. It was a great bonding time. Then I decided to show him how to kick the ball into the goal. Dylan watched me carefully as I came up to the ball and kicked it as hard as I could. The ball was supposed to go across the yard toward the makeshift goalposts we had built, but that's not what happened.

As I approached the ball, my foot slipped to the right. Instead of sailing through the goalposts, the ball hit Dylan directly in the face! I can still see the entire scene in slow motion: the white and black ball traveling through the air, the panic on Dylan's face, the direct hit on his mouth. Then the worst part of all: his two front teeth literally flying from his mouth.

I ran to Dylan's side as the tears streamed down his face and blood trickled from his mouth. With my arms around him, I comforted Dylan and apologized profusely. "I'm so sorry. I didn't mean to hurt you. I'll never do it again."

Dylan calmed down, and together we searched the lawn for his two front teeth, which fortunately were only baby teeth. Then we climbed into the car and drove to the local ice cream parlor. (There's nothing like a double-scoop ice cream cone to wipe away a son's tears and relieve a father's guilt.) On the way I said, "Dylan, you know I didn't mean to hurt you like that, don't you?"

Dylan smiled a large, toothless grin and put his hand on my shoulder. "I know, Dad," he said. "You probably just thought I was a lot faster and could get out of the way." Then he paused for just a moment. "Besides, you just aren't that good at kicking goals."

Apologizing knocks on the door of your children's hearts. It tells them that you want to have a good relationship. It's so easy to wound or discourage our kids, squashing their spirits and hurting their feelings, sometimes without even realizing we're doing it. So be quick to apologize, even if you think they are overreacting. Here are some basic principles that might help:

① Take responsibility.
② Be specific.
③ Watch your tone of voice.
④ Don't place blame or make excuses.
⑤ Say you are sorry.
⑥ Be sensitive and sincere.
⑦ Listen to their feelings and perspective.
⑧ Say, "Will you forgive me?"
⑨ If they aren't ready to forgive, don't push.
⑩ If they are ready, thank them.

By following these principles, you can solve difficulties before they build into a wall of resentment and misunderstanding—a wall that might take years to break down.

Nine-year-old Loren knew he wasn't supposed to use his dad's hammer without permission. So when the hammer was missing and Loren couldn't remember where he'd left it, Dad was furious. Stomping toward the house, Dad shoved past Loren with a strong push that sent him sailing across the yard into a mud puddle. Loren knew he had been wrong to lose the hammer, and he believed that he probably deserved a stronger punishment than landing in a puddle. But what happened next came as a total surprise. Today, some sixty years later, Loren is still moved when he remembers his father coming to his side, lifting him out of the mud, and saying, "I am so sorry. Christians don't act like that." If only we were all so quick to apologize.

ACT ON IT

A true apology requires some change in behavior. An apology that's followed by continued negative attitudes, words, or actions is meaningless. When you make a mistake, it's important to make a repair or restitution. A *repair* fixes the situation. Most situations can be repaired if you are willing to spend the time and energy to do it. Yet if you've missed the opportunity or the damage is too deep, you need to consider *restitution*. Restitution involves giving or doing something sacrificial to show that you take what you did seriously.

As you face your own mistakes, you'll also find it easier to accept your children's mistakes. You'll realize that just as you aren't perfect, neither are they. As you deal with your own failures, you will find yourself more sensitive and patient with their failures. Mistakes are opportunities to learn the importance of:

- keeping your word

- listening to one another

- spending quality time together

- considering consequences

- watching your words

- being less reactive

- evaluating your priorities

- paying attention

I try to learn something from every failure and mistake. For as the old adage goes, "Those who do not learn from the past are destined to repeat it."

Sometimes as we deal with the difficulties of family life, we just aren't sure what to do or how to handle a situation. We may feel overwhelmed or out of control, and we may even need to seek outside help. This is normal. Needing help is nothing to be frustrated or embarrassed about. In fact, admitting that you need help may be the smartest thing you can do. When you are too close to a situation, it is easy to lose perspective. So call a friend, buy a book, or set up an appointment with a counselor. A fresh perspective might be all you need to help you get back on track.

NOBODY'S PERFECT

You make mistakes and your children make mistakes. Instead of getting upset at yourself and frustrated with them, consider mistakes as opportunities to pull a family together.

There is a wonderful scene in the 1991 movie *Regarding Henry* in which the main character, played by Harrison Ford, is eating breakfast with his family. He has a reputation for being harsh and easily angered, but he has just had a life-changing experience. During the meal, his daughter spills her orange juice and the family becomes instantly silent.

"Oh, I'm sorry," she says, expecting her father to yell at her. Instead, he smiles.

"That's okay, I do that all the time."

"You do?" she says in amazement.

"Yeah."

Then he reaches forward and tips over his own juice. "See," he says. He grins, and the tension breaks. Suddenly the family experiences a connection and closeness it hasn't had for a long time.

If your goal is for you or your child to be perfect, you need to understand it will never happen. But a mistake doesn't have to be a crisis. It can be a chance for you to build honesty and understanding and closeness. After all, we have all spilled our orange juice.

TODAY'S TOOLS

Prayer

Dear God,

Sometimes I feel like such a loser. I wish I were the perfect parent, but every day I do or say something that isn't the best. Protect my kids from being hurt or damaged by my selfishness, stubbornness, fear, and negativity.

Give me the courage to face my failures and admit my mistakes. Give me the humility to swallow my pride and apologize to my children or my spouse, or maybe both.

Place the words "I'm sorry," "I was wrong," and "Please forgive me" on my tongue. Then empower me to use them when I need to.

Forgive me for my many mistakes, and help me to forgive myself. Thank you for being able to turn my greatest blunders into something beautiful when I place them in your strong and gentle hands.

Amen.

Passage

If we claim to be without sin, we deceive ourselves and the truth is not in us.
1 John 1:8

Practice

① If you could change three mistakes you have made as a parent, what would they be?
② Go to your children and ask them if there is anything you need to apologize for. If they have a valid concern, take responsibility and apologize.
③ Sit down with your spouse or another parent to discuss the lessons you have learned from your three most recent parenting mistakes.

RULE ❸
FIND YOUR GOLDEN MOMENTS

"I JUST DON'T have the time."

We've all said it. We've all felt it.

Life moves so quickly that we frequently don't have the time to invest in our families the way we really want to. But the reality is that we can't afford *not* to invest. Every day, hundreds of activities, obligations, and responsibilities threaten to pull us away from our families. Many of these are good and important things, yet we all have to ask ourselves whether they are the *most* important. In life we must set our priorities, and I believe that family must be one of our top priorities.

Spending time together as a family is wonderful, but one-on-one time with each family member is equally important. I love spending quality time with each one of my kids separately. It doesn't have to be a big production. It can be as simple as talking to Brittany about her dreams, going to the grocery store with Dylan, or playing a game of chess with Dusty. When I spend one-on-one time with each family member, I'm telling them:

- they are important

- what they think is important

- they are loved

- I want to connect with them

- I like to spend time with them

- I value a relationship with them

SEVEN GOLDEN MOMENTS

When connecting with your child, the more time you invest the better. Yet some moments are more powerful than everyday moments. I call these "golden moments"—times when your children are more talkative and more open to your influence than they normally are. These are moments you don't want to miss. Every child is different, but you will find that at least two of these golden moments probably apply to your child:

Wake-up time: Some kids are morning people. This is when they are most open. They wake up ready to talk. They want to talk about what's going to happen today or what happened yesterday.

Send-off time: These children like to connect before they leave the house. They may take a little bit of time to warm up in the morning, but once they are awake, they become talkative. These children often want to talk about worries they have about the day ahead. They also want to make sure everything is okay between the two of you before they leave.

Entry time: When some children return from day care, school, or an event, they like to review what has happened. They might want to share about what they learned, how they feel, or the people they interacted with. They might be excited or disappointed, but if you don't touch base when things are fresh in their minds, they might not share at all.

Table time: Food and conversation just seem to go together. A lot of children find the dinner table a natural place to talk about their day and things that might be bothering them. When food is the focus, it often feels more comfortable to share what's on your heart and mind.

Bedtime: At the end of the day, when they are tired and their defenses are down, some kids are willing to talk about anything. As they unwind they seem to open up, and many parents find this the best time to connect. Some children use conversation at this time as a means of staying up later, but the candid communication is usually worth the lost sleep.

Car time: This is the perfect time to connect with your kids. Whether on the way to the store or on a road trip, they are trapped in the car with you. Turn off the radio, DVD player, or video game, then talk with each other. You might be surprised at how open your kids can be when your eyes are on the road and all the attention isn't on them.

Teaching time: These spontaneous moments can happen anytime. Yet if you don't take advantage of them immediately, you'll miss the opportunity. These times might be triggered by an event, an emotion, or a question, during which your child's heart is more tender and his mind is more open. Teaching times take advantage of daily events and use them to create a connection.

Learn to recognize golden moments with your child. Don't let them pass you by; use them to learn more about your child, to build your relationship, and to increase your influence in his or her life. You have the power to make a difference in your child's life. This power is not gained through lecturing or threatening or demanding but by building a relationship.

ASKING QUESTIONS

The best way to get to know someone is to ask questions. Parents need to be curious. This doesn't mean you should pry, though there may be times when this is necessary. I'm talking about general questions that help you understand your child better. Questions can open your children up or back them into a corner, depending on how you ask them. The best way to get your kids to open up to you is to be casual. Don't expect perfection or precision from your conversation. If your children believe they will disappoint you or anger you, they will not answer. When children feel safe and comfortable, they aren't afraid to talk. In fact, you may not be able to get them to stop.

Here are a few questions to get you started:

- What is your best friend like?

- What is your favorite room in our house? Why?

- If you had three wishes, what would they be?

- What bugs you most in life?

- How would you describe yourself to someone who didn't know you?

- What is your best memory?

- What is your worst memory?

- If we could go anywhere on vacation, where would we go and what would we do?

- How can I pray for you this week?

- What could we do to be better parents and make this a better family?

The art of asking questions is something every parent should attempt to master. It is a bridge that turns your golden moments into positive and powerful links between parent and child.

Asking a question begins a conversation, but truly listening to the answer makes the connection. If your child does not believe you are listening, he will stop talking. Everybody wants to be heard, but it is easier for parents to ignore, interrupt, or correct rather than listen. Golden moments find their meaning when a child shares his or her thoughts and you listen. Choosing to hear is one of the greatest gifts you can give. Be committed to listen, even if the words are trivial, irrational, or emotionally charged. Listening shows that you care, and it leads to a deeper understanding of your child. It also opens the doors to all sorts of conversations that your child might have otherwise been hesitant to explore.

TAKE THE TIME

Life is full of regrets. Too often parents speak to me of opportunities lost. Each year of your child's life is unique and priceless. Once it passes, that time is irretrievable. There are so many things I wish I had done when my children were younger, but I can't go back. Yet what I can do is enjoy each moment that is before me. Because time is precious and there rarely seems to be enough of it, it is so important to get the maximum value out of every minute together. I want to laugh, play, talk, listen, and connect with my kids. Being intentional and determined is a great way to make this happen.

As you find your child's golden moments, consider these two principles:

1. The investment principle: Consistently investing small amounts of time over a long period of time results in an accumulative positive value.
2. The neglect principle: Neglecting to spend time over a long period of time results in an accumulative negative effect.

In the important areas of life, you can't make up for lost time. But you can choose today, this very moment, to start investing in each child individually and together. It's an investment you will never regret.

As I'm writing this, Dusty has just come home from school.

"Dad, let's go to the store."

I hesitate, thinking how much I need to do. Then I remember the two principles above. I don't want to miss another opportunity, and besides, Dusty enjoys car time. I smile, put my arm around his shoulders, and say, "Sure, let's go."

TODAY'S TOOLS

Prayer

Dear God,

> *Open my eyes to my children's golden moments.*
> *Open my ears to really listen during these times.*
> *Open my heart to their hurts and hopes.*
>
> *Remind me daily of the importance of one-on-one time with each of my children. Assist me in turning my good intentions for quality time into a fun-loving reality.*
>
> *When I talk to my kids, plant comfortable questions in my mind that don't sound like interrogations or accusations. Give me a positive curiosity that can open the door to closeness and communication with my kids.*
>
> *Teach me to say no to distractions that keep me from my family and to say yes to my children's golden moments. Remind me that this season of my life belongs to my children. They are my job, my responsibility, my ministry, my love, and my legacy.*
>
> *Open up my life to healthy priorities, so that in the future I will not look back with sadness and regret.*
>
> *Amen.*

Passage

Fix these words of mine in your hearts and minds. . . . Teach them to your children, talking about them when you sit at home and when you walk along the road, when you lie down and when you get up.
Deuteronomy 11:18-19

Practice

① Ask each of your children when they most like to talk to you. Then consider when in the next week you can connect with them during these golden moments.

② Generate your own list of ten questions that you'd like to ask your kids in order to get to know them better.

③ Track how much quality time you spent with your family one-on-one and all together in the past month. Then ask yourself:

Am I satisfied with this?

Are they satisfied with this?

What can I do better?

What opportunities have I missed?

RULE ❹
ENCOURAGE THEM

"WHAT IN THE WORLD were you thinking?"

"I don't know," said six-year-old Nathan.

"How can you not know?" Nathan's father was furious. "Sometimes I don't know what to do with you. Are you ever going to get it? You're impossible!"

Nathan just stood there, not knowing what to do or say. But something broke deep inside. *If Dad doesn't know what to do with me, I must be hopeless. Not only hopeless, but also stupid.*

Years passed, and Nathan never forgot what his father said that night in anger. Those words haunted him and ate away at his confidence. Nathan didn't go out for basketball: "Because I'm no good." He didn't make many friends: "They wouldn't like me." He didn't go to college: "I'm not smart enough." What's sad is that Nathan was an excellent basketball player, his friends respected him, and he was very bright.

Nathan's parents were good people who loved their son deeply. But they had no idea how much their negative attitude, words, actions, and expectations hurt Nathan. They would have done anything for him, but they didn't know how to encourage him.

One of the most important gifts you can ever give your child is the gift of encouragement. In fact, in his book *The 7 Habits of Highly Effective Families*, Stephen Covey writes, "Creating a warm, caring, supportive, encouraging environment is probably the most important thing you can do for your family."

YOUR ATTITUDE

You have heard it a hundred times, and it is true: Attitude is everything. A positive attitude encourages and builds up your children, while a negative attitude quickly tears them down. Yet we live in a broken world surrounded by negatives, so it's easy to absorb this negativity and inadvertently pass it on to our children. The apostle Paul says that love "always protects, always trusts, always hopes, always perseveres" (1 Corinthians 13:7). This advice sounds easy, but since none of us are perfect and none of us have perfect children, it can be quite a challenge to follow Paul's advice.

A you-can-do-it attitude tells your children that you believe in them. So when ten-year-old Brittany told me she wanted to be a mosquito lawyer, I knew better than to shoot down her idea. Instead, I asked, "What does a mosquito lawyer do?"

"She stands up for the rights of mosquitoes," she said. "After all, people smash and kill them without a thought; mosquitoes should have the right to life."

"Brittany, if you want to be a mosquito lawyer, I'm sure you will be the best one in the world." As I spoke, a huge smile spread across my little girl's face.

Attitude is contagious. If I am positive with my children, they will usually be positive in return. An encouraging attitude can show itself in patience, a smile, or a cheerful tone of voice. A positive attitude says, "You are fantastic!" A negative attitude says, "You can't do it." If I am negative with my kids, they will reflect my negativity. This breeds discouragement, frustration, and depression.

A negative attitude is a terrible trap that often becomes a self-fulfilling prophecy. Such an attitude:

- focuses on the negative

- anticipates the negative

- talks about the negative

- magnifies the negative

- holds on to the negative

- can't see beyond the negative

- believes the future will be negative

The bottom line is that a negative attitude places shackles on you and your children. Negativity prevents all of you from being happy and healthy.

YOUR WORDS

Words are far more powerful than most people ever realize.

Words can tear your children down—diminishing, depressing, and minimizing them. Negative words can be very destructive weapons. Yet parents can so easily to slip into the habit of using negative phrases such as:

"Can't you do anything right?"

"Who do you think you are?"

"You never listen."

"I've had it with you."

"You'll never amount to anything."

"You are so lazy."

"Don't you take care of anything?"

"What's wrong with you?"

"You'll be the death of me yet!"

These types of words are poison. Yet there is hope. If you take responsibility for saying something negative, your children will most likely forgive you. Your words may still leave scars, but your apology will soften the blow. Once you apologize, give them some positive words, remembering that it takes approximately eight positives to make up for every negative.

Just as negative words can tear children down, positive words can build your children up—engaging, empowering, and inspiring them. Gary Smalley writes, "Affirming words from moms and dads are like light switches. Speak a word of affirmation at the right moment in a child's life and it's like lighting up a whole roomful of possibilities." Positive words are life giving. Every day, make it a point to use encouraging words with your child. Say things like:

"That's great."

"You do that so well."

"I love your attitude."

"I am so glad you are my child."

"Good job!"

"You're incredible!"

"You look fantastic."

"I'm proud of you."

"You have such a nice smile."

"You have a great personality."

Catch your children in the act of doing something good—a good attitude, a good word, a good deed—and encourage them immediately and specifically. King Solomon wrote, "An anxious heart weighs a man down, but a kind word cheers him up" (Proverbs 12:25). When you praise your child, you will both feel more positive. When children are praised, they are more likely to repeat whatever elicited the praise. They are also more likely to learn confidence, appreciation, and self-respect. Words are powerful. The words you say can reach to the very core of your child, strengthening his spirit or hardening his heart. Words can travel with your child for years, maybe his entire life, encouraging or discouraging him. So every day, look for ways to praise your child.

YOUR ACTIONS

Words are important, but it's also true that actions speak louder than words. Make sure that what you do is consistent with what you say. When talking to your child, face her and look into her eyes. If she's small, get down to her level. Encouraging actions show interest, respect, and love. Be careful that your body language doesn't contradict what you want to communicate. Those little things, such as having an open posture, leaning toward her, being relaxed, and smiling, can make all the difference in the world.

Encouraging actions also involve following through with what you say. If you promise your child a fishing trip or a bike ride, make sure it happens. Children have incredible memories. They will remember promises you've made long after you've forgotten them. A broken promise tells your child that you don't believe he's that important. And as one twelve-year-old boy told me, "If you aren't important to your own dad, you're probably not important to anybody."

Keeping your word, even when it's difficult, is incredibly encouraging to your family. It not only shows that you love them, but it lets them know that you are trustworthy. In a world full of frustrations and disappointments, a child needs to know that when all else fails, her parents can be trusted.

Finally, pair your encouraging words with healthy, affirming touch. Studies show that lack of touch causes people to withdraw, shrivel up, and perhaps even die. Touch means everything to a child. So when your kids are young, make it a point to hold hands, snuggle, kiss their cheeks and foreheads, tickle, and wrap your arms around them. When they are older, keep close without crowding them. Give them hugs, put your hand on their shoulders, and walk beside them. Even when they push you away, don't go too far. Often it's the children who seem the most un-huggable who need hugs the most. All children need regular touch, but in times of crisis or difficulty, they need it even more. So try your best to offer a shoulder to cry on whenever necessary.

Displays of physical affection come naturally to some people but are difficult and uncomfortable to others. Some people can give but find it hard to receive. Others can receive but feel awkward when giving. In these situations, I apply the "pat principle": When in doubt, pat. Gently pat their heads, knees, hands, shoulders, or backs, letting them know that you are there and you honestly care.

BE THEIR CHEERLEADER

"Stop!" yelled the police officer.

I was only walking down the aisle of the local supermarket, but I stopped. The police officer came up to me and gave me a big bear hug.

"Dr. Steve, thank you so much."

I stared at this man in his midtwenties and thought, *Who in the world is this?*

The officer chuckled. "You don't recognize me, do you?"

"I'm sorry, but I don't," I said with a bit of embarrassment.

"Ten years ago," the officer began, "my parents brought me to see you because I was adrift and not headed anywhere in my life. I only saw you three or four times, but in one of our times together I told you that I wanted to be a cop. You told me you thought I'd be a great cop. I went home that day and thought, *If Dr. Steve says I'd be a great cop, I think I can do it.*

"As the years passed, most people thought I'd give up, but I kept remembering what you told me. If you hadn't encouraged me, I don't know where I'd be today. So thank you!"

We all need someone sitting in the stands cheering us on, telling us we can do it, letting us know that we are loved, no matter what. I know my children aren't perfect, but I also know they hold amazing potential. I want to do all I can to nurture, reassure, inspire, and motivate my children. As James Dobson wrote: "It's better to make a child stretch to reach your high opinion than stoop to match your disrespect."

I learned an incredible lesson from the police officer in the supermarket that day: Encouragement can change a person's life, and it's really not that hard to do.

TODAY'S TOOLS

Prayer

Dear God,

This world can get so negative and so can I. There are days when nothing seems to go the way I want. This is when I get discouraged and can easily pass my negativity on to my children.

Help me to stop this destructive pattern.

Build in me a positive, uplifting, encouraging spirit. Create in me a clean heart that is clear of negativity, insensitivity, or discouragement.

Encourage me to praise my kids every opportunity I get. Show me how to encourage them with my attitude, words, and actions.

Give me a you-can-do-it attitude.

Give me powerfully affirming words.

Give me warm and caring actions.

Show me how to be the most active and encouraging cheerleader in my children's lives.

Thank you for all the times you have encouraged me when I was down, frustrated, alone, stuck, or feeling bad. Teach me to do the same for my kids.

Amen.

Passage

Encourage one another and build each other up.

1 Thessalonians 5:11

Practice

① Ask your spouse or a good friend how encouraging a person you are. Have them rate your attitude, words, and actions. Then have them give you examples of when they have seen you be encouraging and discouraging.

② Make a list of ten positive statements you want to say to each of your children. Commit to saying one of these each day for the next ten days.

③ Look for opportunities to give your children healthy, affirming physical touch—hugs, kisses, or pats on the back.

RULE ❺
HAVE FUN

SUMMERS WERE ALWAYS the best when I was a kid.

School was out, the days were warm, and the world was waiting to be conquered. Some days my buddies and I climbed on our bikes and rode to the edges of the neighborhood. On other days we'd swim, hike, play ball, build forts, climb trees, and do whatever else sounded like fun. The possibilities were as great as our imaginations. The world was full of wonder and excitement. In those days, my only job was to have fun.

Then I grew up. I got married. We had children. Suddenly life got busy—filled with responsibilities, pressures, and obligations. Now there seems to be little or no time for fun. It's easy to become way too serious and maybe even a little bit dull. Where is the fun, the excitement, the wonder? Every family needs to have fun.

Parents can learn a lot from their children. Kids know how to have fun. They love to play and laugh. Parents need to relearn how important fun is and give themselves permission to have more playtime. We can begin by watching our kids having fun. Remember what it was like when we were their age? I know chores and studies are important, but fun is equally important. Consider some of these advantages of family fun:

① It eases stress.
② It builds togetherness.
③ It stretches creativity.
④ It promotes laughter.
⑤ It adds excitement.
⑥ It fights boredom.
⑦ It builds great memories.

Your family needs to regularly set aside time to play and have as much fun as you possibly can.

FAMILY NIGHTS

"What do you like best about your family?" I asked eight-year-old Ryan.

"Family night," he said without hesitation.

"So tell me about family night."

"Every Tuesday is game night, and every Friday is movie night." Ryan smiled brightly. "They're the best nights of my life."

I still remember with great fondness sitting beside my father after supper as he read *The Swiss Family Robinson* aloud. Family nights come in all sorts of unique and individual styles. Here are some ideas to get you started:

Hobby night: Enjoy a sport or hobby together, such as bowling, tennis, basketball, photography, or baking. If you don't have a hobby, try something new.

Workout night: Set aside an evening for family exercise. Go to a gym or work out at home. Do aerobics or lift weights.

Music night: Family sing-alongs used to be very popular, and they can still be fun. Or if any family members play a musical instrument, have a family concert.

Television night: Find a special television show that you all enjoy. Make a big deal about it. Fix popcorn or some great treat and watch the program together.

Favorite food night: Schedule a night that each family member, on a rotating basis, gets to select his or her favorite food or restaurant.

Guest night: Invite a friend, neighbor, relative, or coworker to spend an evening with your family. This is a great opportunity to get to know others better.

Reading night: Children, no matter what age, like to hear a good story. Start when they are babies and read right through their teens. This is a great way to bond and also to create lifelong readers.

Choose-your-activity night: This is a chance for each family member, from youngest to oldest, to choose an activity for the evening (within reason). The one rule is that everybody has to join in, with no complaining.

Another country night: Spend an evening learning about another country. If you know a family from that country, invite them over. Eat food that's native to the country you're learning about, sing local songs, tell cultural stories, and discover facts about the people who live there.

Game night: Almost everybody loves a game night. Discover what games your family enjoys most—tic-tac-toe, hide-and-seek, checkers, chess, cards, Yahtzee, or Monopoly—then have fun.

No matter what you do, family night will be a tradition you will never regret and your children will never forget.

BIGGER EVENTS

I start thinking about the weekend about four o'clock every Wednesday afternoon. It isn't that I don't like my job, but I do want to be prepared.

I want something special to happen every weekend. As you can tell, I'm intentional about having fun. I listen to what other families are doing, I read the local newspaper for ideas, and I think back on what I thought was the most fun when I was young. By Friday I usually have something in mind for a great weekend. My ideas often fall into one of the following categories.

Active events: These include swimming, canoeing, hiking, snowshoeing, bike riding, playing sports, or camping.

Entertainment events: We might go to a baseball game, circus, play, concert, movie, museum, or zoo.

Adventure events: This is when you set out to explore something new—a park, a city, a trail, a road, or anything you've never explored before.

Home events: Sometimes a big event can happen at home by baking cookies, flying kites, making forts, or building something together.

Any of these activities can be great fun. I've learned a lot of lessons from my kids. One of them is that fun doesn't have to be expensive. Years ago Tami and I took two of our children to Disneyland. It was a wonderful vacation, and after each day I'd ask the kids, "What was your favorite activity today?"

Seven-year-old Brittany said Toon Town one day, Splash Mountain on another, and shopping on the final afternoon. Five-year-old Dylan loved Tom Sawyer Island, It's a Small World, and Mr. Toad's Wild Ride.

As we settled into our seats and prepared for the airplane flight home, I turned to Dylan and asked, "What was your favorite activity of the whole trip?"

He smiled and quickly replied, "The cart."

"The cart?" I responded. "I don't remember any carts."

"Dad, you remember."

"No, I don't, Dylan. I'm sorry, but I don't remember any carts."

In frustration he explained, "Remember when you put all our bags on the metal cart at the airport? Then you dropped them off at the counter and let me ride the cart back to where it belonged? You made it go so fast that I had to really hold on tight." With a huge grin he said, "That was the best part of the whole trip. Thanks, Dad."

I leaned back in my seat and thought to myself, *The next time Dylan wants a fun trip, I won't worry about taking him to Disneyland. I'll just drive to the local airport, drop my quarters in the cart dispenser, and spend the afternoon pushing him around the halls in a luggage cart!*

Kids sometimes get the most joy out of the simplest, most inexpensive things: an empty refrigerator box, a wooden stick, a handful of multicolored marbles, or even an airport luggage cart.

Another lesson my kids have taught me is that what's fun for an adult isn't always fun for kids. Not long ago I took my two boys to New York City to show them the sights. We visited the Statue of Liberty, the Empire State Building, Times Square, and Ground Zero. "Isn't this great?" I said with enthusiasm. "It's okay," they said halfheartedly. I was having a great time, but they were bored stiff. Then I took them to Central Park, where they discovered a large outcropping of metamorphic rock. "Dad, this is fantastic!" my boys shouted. For the next hour and a half they climbed on the rocks and declared, "This makes the whole trip worth it!"

Quite honestly, I wanted to explore Central Park, but sometimes as a parent you just have to do it their way. It was fun to watch them run and play and climb.

Bigger events don't have to be complicated or expensive; they just have to be fun. Sometimes the best way to know what your kids would enjoy is to ask them. They'll tell you, I promise. Bigger events sometimes involve the whole family, but they don't always have to. There are times I do things one-on-one with my kids. Then there are times when I take the boys and Tami takes Brittany or when Tami takes the older two and I take Dustin. Creative divisions can make your bigger events even more enjoyable.

LOVE AND LAUGHTER

To watch my family having fun is one of my greatest joys as a parent. Life can be difficult, but laughter makes things a little more bearable. We are a family that loves to laugh. Yes, we are silly at times, and our jokes are rather immature, but when we laugh together it feels as if everything is okay. Just as I was writing this, Dustin sneezed and I said, "Wow!" He sneezed again and I said, "Double Wow!" Dustin gave me a why-in-the-world-did-you-say-that look and burst out laughing. Suddenly we were both laughing. Solomon once wrote that "a cheerful heart is good medicine" (Proverbs 17:22), and who can argue with Solomon?

TODAY'S TOOLS

Prayer

Dear God,

Life can get so busy and hectic that sometimes I forget to stop and enjoy it. Help me to watch my kids have fun and to stop what I'm doing so I can join them. Send me to their side.

Encourage us to play together, dance together, sing together, laugh together, and have a wonderful time together.

Show me how to smile more and laugh more. Fill my mind with things to do that will bring us closer together.

Show me how to relax and set things aside so I can connect with my kids. Forgive me for taking things so seriously that I miss opportunities to let my family know how much I love them.

Give me a light and playful heart. Teach me to have fun.

Amen.

Passage

There is a time for everything . . . a time to laugh . . . a time to dance.
Ecclesiastes 3:1, 4

Practice

① Sit down with your family and schedule a family night once a week for the next two months. Then assign each member of your family an equal number of nights to plan whatever they would like to do on their night (as long as it is safe, legal, and within budget and meets your approval).

② Come up with a big event you can do sometime in the next three months. Consider these ideas:

> *active events*

> *entertainment events*

adventure events

home events

Once you figure out what you want to do, mark it on the calendar, but don't tell the kids what it is. Keep it a surprise until the last moment.

③ Rent a humorous DVD or find a book of funny stories, then sit together in your family room and let yourselves laugh and laugh and laugh.

RULE ❻
GET TO KNOW EACH OTHER

FAMILIES ARE SO BUSY, we sometimes miss the obvious.

When Dylan was ten, he got injured playing indoor soccer. His arm hurt, but we figured that's what happens in sports. We told him to relax and it would feel better in a few days. Life went on and we all forgot about Dylan's arm—everybody but Dylan. Four days later he came to us. "My arm still hurts. I can't even move it." We took Dylan to the doctor and discovered it was broken.

If we had paid attention, we would have known that this was more than just a sore arm. If we had been more alert, we'd have noticed that Dylan was more withdrawn than usual and that he was protecting his arm. We should have remembered that Dylan doesn't complain unless the pain is high. Yet when life gets hectic, we often don't see what is right in front of us.

Too many families spend time together but don't really know each other. We may know what's on the surface, but we don't dig deep enough to understand who the others really are. If we did, we'd see that each member of a family is incredibly special and amazingly unique—a combination of similarities and differences. I've often been asked, "How can children from the same family be so different?" The answer is that children have:

- different birth orders

- different emotional makeups

- different experiences

- different physical capabilities

- different personalities

- different mental capacities

- different genetic codes

One of the biggest mistakes parents make is to treat their children all the same. This seems, on the surface, to be the most fair and simple method of parenting. But it is neither fair nor simple. It also keeps us from truly getting to know our kids.

Each of us, regardless of our age, yearns to be known and understood. It is lonely to feel like people don't understand us, especially people in our own family. A great family takes the time and energy to know one another. They pay attention to each other. They don't make assumptions or jump to conclusions. Here are six areas we should all work on to better understand those we love.

THEIR STRENGTHS

Each member of your family has a set of strengths, talents, and abilities—things they are naturally good at. I want to know each of my children's strengths so I can compliment and encourage them. In order to compliment your kids, you first need to identify their talents. Your child may be good at:

- communication

- sports

- creativity

- friendliness

- kindness

- schoolwork

- hard work

- positive attitude

- memorization

- music

This is far from a complete list. Watch your children while they work or play or interact with others. Soon you will discover what they are good at. Then you can begin to compliment each family member's strengths. Point out any time you see someone using his or her talents. Or you may simply say, "You are such a creative person" or "I keep noticing how kind you are" or "I am so impressed by your incredible ability to remember things." Lastly, encourage and reward your spouse and children for their abilities.

THEIR WEAKNESSES

None of us are perfect. We all have things we do well and things we struggle with. As you recognize your children's strengths, it's also important to know their weaknesses. This is not to embarrass, pressure, or harass them, but so that you can stand beside them. As a parent, I want to emphasize their strengths and be patient with their weaknesses. I push them to build upon their strengths, and I assist them as they compensate for their weaknesses. There are even times I might give a child a break and reduce my expectations because I know that an area is a weakness.

Strengths and weaknesses are a part of being human. Your child has both. In fact, most of us have more weaknesses than strengths. It is important to assist your children if their area of weakness involves a crucial life skill, such as reading, problem solving, or basic hygiene. But if their weakness is in a less crucial area—sports, music, or advanced chemistry—you might just relax and let it go. Always define your children by their strengths, not their weaknesses. Acknowledge areas of difficulty only in order to understand them and help them.

THEIR NEEDS

We all have needs. Different personalities have different needs, and at different stages of life our needs might change. As you know your family's individual needs, you can be more sensitive to them and help meet their needs. There is nothing wrong with having needs; it's the way we are built. Some common needs include:

- security

- acceptance

- achievement

- order

- freedom

- peace

- variety

As we know each other's needs, we start to understand what makes our family tick and what makes them happy. If we don't know each family member's needs, it will be difficult to connect with them on a personal level. When we are aware of and sensitive to their needs, our children feel affirmed by us.

THEIR FEARS

Fears can feel overwhelming at any age. Tami is afraid of spiders. She is fascinated by snakes, lizards, and mice, but the tiniest spider will drive her to panic. Fears are not always rational, but they are real. So when Tami screams for help, I don't lecture her on the harmlessness of spiders. I simply remove the spider, and she is grateful.

Knowing your children's fears gives you an opportunity to come alongside them and be a source of comfort. When children are left alone with their fears, they begin to worry and grow anxious. Your presence can be very calming. Rather than getting frustrated, reassure them gently and confidently. Listen to their fears and talk to them. Put your arm around them and pray with them. Remind them that God is always close and he always cares. Reassure them that there is always a way out of scary situations. You might even tell them what scared you when you were their age and how you worked through it. Fear is a wonderful opportunity for closeness between parent and child.

THEIR HURTS

Life can be cruel, and children are tender, especially in the face of difficulties. What is challenging for an adult can be overwhelming to a child. Sometimes children don't know how to talk about their struggles or they are too embarrassed, so they hide their hurts.

One day I asked Dusty, "When did you feel the greatest hurt?" He related a story about telling his friends a joke. They didn't seem to get the joke and asked, "What are you saying?" Dusty felt as if his friends were making fun of him. He said it took him a few days to figure out that they couldn't understand his words because of his speech impediment. "Then I felt stupid because I couldn't even talk right," he told me. We went on to discuss how hard that was and how glad he was that he had overcome the speech problem. Dusty's friends had left a scar, but if we hadn't had this discussion I would have never known how deeply it hurt him. Other areas of potential hurt your children might be dealing with include:

- death

- divorce

- embarrassment or shame

- rejection or neglect

- abuse

- negativity

- failure

- trauma

- conflict

- sickness or injury

When you know your children's hurts, you are better able to offer them compassion and comfort.

THEIR INTERESTS

Knowing your children's interests pulls you into their lives by giving you a peek into their hearts and minds. Every child has interests and preferences and passions. These may be quite different from yours, but because you love your children and want a positive relationship with them, you climb into their world. Study your children, watch them, play with them, and interact with them. Ask yourself:

What does my child love to do?

What brings a smile to his face?

What does she talk about?

What does he spend the most time and money on?

Knowing your children's interests is only the first step. The next is to join them. If they love soccer, go to soccer games. If they like to play board games, set up the Monopoly board. Make it fun and get into it. If you do these things out of obligation or duty, your child will see right through you. Brittany loves dance, and she is on the high school dance team. So I attend dance competitions. At first I was hesitant, but then I saw her passion. Brittany is a great dancer, and her team is incredible. Dylan enjoys music, so last summer we drove five hours to an outdoor music festival. For three days we sat in 110-degree heat and listened to some remarkable music. Dusty is fascinated with World War II, so we watch movies and specials about the war. I've bought him books about the subject, and we've also had the opportunity to meet with several World War II soldiers. As I join with my children around their interests, we develop a link that I hope will last the rest of our lives.

TAKE NOTICE

Andrea is an energetic, bright fifteen-year-old who ran away from home. When I asked why she left, she said, "I'm not important to my parents."

"What makes you think that?" I asked.

"My parents don't have time for me," she said angrily. "They don't even know who I am."

Sadly enough, Andrea was right. Her parents were so busy providing nice things and a nice environment that they hadn't spent much time with Andrea. As we talked, tears began to flow down this young lady's face. She told me about her hurts and fears.

"Do you think your parents don't care?"

"I don't know," she said.

I knew Andrea's parents loved her; they just didn't know how to show her. So I sat down with them and explained how their daughter felt. They were shocked. We talked about what a wonderful, creative girl Andrea is. We discussed her strengths, her needs, and her interests.

Over the next six months, Andrea and her parents experienced a marvelous healing. Now they spend time together on a regular basis doing all sorts of fun things.

"It's so exciting," Andrea told me recently. "It's like my parents really understand me, and I'm beginning to understand them. I feel sorry about what I put them through, but I'm happy they didn't give up on me. Now I know beyond a doubt that they love me."

Knowing our children is one of the best ways to say "I love you."

TODAY'S TOOLS

Prayer

Dear God,

Thank you for knowing all there is to know about me and still loving me. You know my past and my future. You know all my words and ways. You even know my innermost secrets and how many hairs I have on my head. Help me to seek to know my children with the same passion with which you know me.

Teach me to celebrate and compliment my children's strengths.

Show me how to encourage my children as they struggle to accept and deal with their weaknesses.

Make me aware of their various needs and how I might help to meet them.

Prod me to take their fears seriously, standing beside them and comforting them.

Give me a soft and sympathetic heart when their hurts seem overwhelming.

Inspire me to make my children's interests my interests so I can share their fascinations and joys.

Keep me open to continuing to know my children as they grow and change and mature.

Amen.

Passage

O LORD, you have searched me and you know me. You know when I sit and when I rise; you perceive my thoughts from afar.
Psalm 139:1-2

Practice

1. List all the ways in which the members of your family are different from each other. Get everybody together and discuss whether everyone agrees with your list.
2. Write a short note to each one of your children, sharing three specific strengths you see in them.
3. Tell your children either your greatest fear or your deepest hurt. Then tell them how you have learned to deal with this.
4. Ask each person in your family what his or her most important interests are. Schedule an event or discussion that pertains to each person's interest.

RULE **❼**
MOTIVATE WORK

KIDS HATE WORK.

They want to play, watch TV, spend time with friends, and do anything but work. Most kids don't instinctively clean their rooms, make their beds, pick up their toys, or wash their dishes. I feel as if I'm constantly reminding my kids to clean their rooms. I probably drive them crazy, but I know this is about something bigger than just having a clean room.

Most children and teenagers seem committed to find every conceivable way to avoid work. It's up to the parents to teach life skills and responsibility. Since work is a big part of life maturity, children and parents are bound to run into some conflict in this area. But don't give up; this is important.

Successful people have learned how to work hard. They realize that anything worthwhile in life requires a certain amount of effort, determination, and work. If you do nothing, you usually get nothing. These are important lessons that every child needs to learn. The bottom line is that hard work is a good thing. There is joy and satisfaction to be gained when we put forth strong, serious effort toward a goal. Few things feel better than finishing a task and sitting back to enjoy a job well done.

Yet in our current culture we want things to be easy. We want the same for our kids. We want them to have some of the benefits and experiences we never had. So we give freely until our children begin to take for granted all the benefits of hard work without putting in the effort. It is good to be generous with our children, but there are serious consequences to being too generous. Inadvertently we teach passivity, laziness, entitlement, and disappointment. Hard work has many advantages, such as the following:

1. It builds a can-do attitude.
2. It teaches responsibility.
3. It develops skills.
4. It overcomes laziness.
5. It accomplishes tasks.
6. It enriches character.
7. It teaches us to appreciate effort.
8. It keeps us from trouble.
9. It assists others.
10. It strengthens self-esteem.

These ten advantages will benefit your children throughout their lives. Since hard work rarely comes naturally, parents must learn how to motivate their children to work.

EVERYDAY CHORES

All children need to be assigned household chores. It is not healthy or positive for you to do everything yourself, although it might seem easier and more efficient at times. Daily tasks show children that they have value and that all family members must work together to make a household run smoothly.

Here are some basic strategies that you can use to get your kids involved in helping around the house.

Start early: The earlier children learn to work, the more likely it will become a pattern in their life. Starting early will also make them less resistant to working when they get older.

Show them how: Children need to know exactly what is expected of them. Give them simple and specific steps for completing each task. Then show them how to do it.

Be age appropriate: Different jobs can be done at different ages. As children grow and develop, they can be given additional and more challenging chores. For example, preschoolers can pick up toys, grade-schoolers can clear the table, and high schoolers can do laundry.

Model work: Let your kids see you work, either on your own chores or with them. Show them that chores are something that everybody in the family does.

Create routines: Set up certain days of the week or times during the day to do chores. Then be consistent with maintaining this chore routine.

Make it visual: Make a chart that includes all the family chores and who is responsible for each task. Then post it where the kids will see it daily. Also write out any check-off lists or contracts that might help get things done.

Make it positive: When possible, turn chores into games or contests. Smiling, laughing, and singing can help to make chores feel a lot less like work. Even boring or difficult chores don't have to be drudgery.

Encourage teamwork: Work together in pairs or as an entire family on certain chores. With others involved, difficult tasks seem much easier and can be accomplished more quickly.

Provide logical consequences: If your children forget or refuse to do their assigned chores, don't yell, nag, or threaten. Simply apply the logical or previously agreed-upon consequence.

Don't expect perfection: Few children will do a chore as well as you do. Remember, children are in process. To expect perfection, or even excellence, is to be disappointed.

Each of these strategies is helpful, but the most important is yet to come. The most powerful way to motivate work is to reward your children for chores well done. Praise and encouragement almost always motivate kids to try harder and work longer. Verbal affirmation is the greatest tool you have. Let them know how much you appreciate their attitude and effort. Compliment them for some aspect of what they have done. Tell them that you are proud of them. Other ways to reward your children include prizes, privileges, money, or fun family times.

SPECIAL PROJECTS

Outside the regular routine of everyday chores, special projects have their own unique qualities. Each special project has its own flavor: Some are fun and some are grueling, some can be done quickly and others seem to drag on for months.

In our family, we have certain tasks that are *yearly projects*. Each June we have the despised "Bark Dust Day," though it rarely seems to get done in a day. This is when Tami and I and the three kids spend from early morning until sunset pulling weeds from the flower gardens and spreading bark dust over them. It's a miserable job, but when it's done, the gardens sure look great. Then each November, usually the day after Thanksgiving, we have "Christmas Lights Day." Tami and Brittany pull out the Christmas boxes and start decorating the inside of the house while the boys and I hang strand after strand of holiday lights on the outside of the house. This is a wonderful day. We all work hard, and we all have fun together as a family.

Then there are one-of-a-kind projects. These are projects that might involve improvements or repairs. Several summers ago, all five of us worked for more than a month building a cobblestone patio. Other projects offer a chance for one-on-one time together. Tami helped Brittany paint her room. Dusty and I built a water feature in our backyard with a fountain bubbling out of a piece of granite. Dylan and I went out one cold January day and cut up a tree that had fallen in a windstorm. All of these are one-of-a-kind projects that have made our relationships stronger and our family life better.

The most satisfying are the reaching-out projects. This is when we do something to help others. My fifteen-year-old neighbor, Nick, mows the lawn for an elderly lady and a single mother. He doesn't get paid; he just does it. Tami and the kids periodically fix meals for families who are experiencing sickness or who have just had a baby. When Brittany was fourteen, she and I spent a week in Mexico pouring concrete floors in small houses built on a garbage pit. Working to help others might not be easy, but my kids will tell you that it is always worth it.

The more you work on special projects with your family, the more natural it becomes. When the children were younger, Tami and I were always the ones to introduce special projects. Now my kids are just as likely to suggest a project as we are. The projects we have done together have given us delightful memories.

Just the other day Dusty asked me, "Dad, when I get older will you come over and help me with my projects? Or will you still need me to help you?"

I smiled and said, "Maybe we should both help each other."

"Yes," Dusty said, "we can help each other. It will go a lot faster that way."

"YOU WORK WITH ME, AND I'LL WORK WITH YOU"

Hard work is a skill I want to build into my children's lives. Solomon wrote, "The desires of the diligent are fully satisfied" (Proverbs 13:4), and I want my kids to be satisfied. I want them to learn the advantages of diligent work. One of the phrases I frequently use with my kids is, "You work with me, and I'll work with you."

Whenever we have an everyday chore or a special project to do and I sense any hesitation, I just use this simple phrase. It often motivates them. When they have cooperated, I'll smile and say, "Since you worked with me, I want to work with you." Then we'll go out for ice cream or do something they like. But when they don't join in and work hard, I'll calmly say, "I'm sorry, but you didn't work with me." Then they lose something—such as television time, an event they wanted to attend, or a visit from a friend.

"Dad, will you help me sort my LEGOs into different colors?" Dusty asked the other day.

"Let me see," I said. "Have you been working with me?"

"Yep," he said, "I helped you mow the lawn yesterday, and this morning I made my bed."

I sat down beside him and said, "Then I had better work with you." Together we created piles of red, blue, black, white, yellow, and gray LEGOs. And we had a great time!

I love to work with my kids, and most of the time they work with me. As parents motivate their kids to work, families get closer.

TODAY'S TOOLS

Prayer

Dear God,

For six days you worked, and on the seventh day you rested. Show me the proper balance between work and play, drivenness and rest, responsibility and relaxation.

Encourage me to work beside my children, showing them how to work hard and do a good job. Help me to motivate them to have a good attitude toward work.

Forgive me for the times I have failed to teach them the importance of chores, doing their best, following through, and being responsible.

Help me to be firm and persistent to get my kids started on work. Help me to be calm and patient as they are doing their work. Help me to be full of praise and encouragement when they have finished their work.

Remind all of us that work is simply a part of life and that once it is done we can play.

Amen.

Passage

Lazy hands make a man poor, but diligent hands bring wealth. He who gathers crops in summer is a wise son. . . . Diligent hands will rule. . . . All hard work brings a profit.

Proverbs 10:4-5; 12:24; 14:23

Practice

① Establish at least three age-appropriate chores for each of your children. Write them down and post them in a place your children will see them daily.

② Determine the reward for a job well done. Be sure to celebrate after hard work.

③ Set up a reaching-out project in which you spend a morning or afternoon doing work for others. It may be helping a neighbor, an elderly person, a school, a charitable organization, or a person who is ill.

RULE ❽
DISCIPLINE FAIRLY

"HONEY, DO NOT TOUCH that plant."

Two-year-old Brittany reached out with her left hand and touched the plant.

I sat down on the floor in front of her, looked her in the eye, and calmly asked, "Did you hear what I just said?"

"Yes, Daddy."

"Then if you touch the plant again," I said, still calmly, "I'm going to have to swat your hand."

Brittany looked me in the eye, reached out, and touched the plant.

It was a test and I knew it. Brittany was saying, *I can do what I want, and you can't stop me.*

I gently took her left hand in mine and said, "I asked you not to touch the plant, but you disobeyed. So I need to swat this hand." Then I firmly swatted her little hand with two fingers.

Brittany stared at me in disbelief, with huge tears forming in her beautiful brown eyes.

"Honey, I love you," I said, "but I need you to obey me. So please don't touch the plant."

Without hesitation Brittany reached out and touched the plant. I couldn't believe it! I think that was the moment I knew for sure that Brittany was a strong-willed child. I swallowed my anger and said to myself, *This is a teaching opportunity. Stay calm and follow through with what you said. Don't overreact.*

"Brittany, I'm sorry you did that," I said. "Now I have to swat your hand again."

I gently took her hand and swatted it a little harder with my two fingers. She burst into tears and opened her arms for me to hold her. We hugged for a few minutes and then I asked, "What happens when you don't mind?"

"It hurts," she said, pointing to her hand.

Children need firm, consistent limits. They also need to learn that there are consequences when they go beyond these limits. Therefore discipline is critical to a great family. Solomon wrote, "Discipline your son, and he will give you peace; he will bring delight to your soul" (Proverbs 29:17). The word *discipline* comes from a root word that means "to teach." Parents discipline their children in order to teach them responsibility, knowing that a disciplined child is more likely to be successful as an adult. An undisciplined child tends to be out of control, making choices and establishing patterns that will haunt him the rest of his life.

Healthy parents discipline their children because they love them. Yet most children hate discipline and will fight against it. They will hide, yell, threaten, challenge, make you feel guilty—anything to avoid facing discipline. As a parent, you must be fair, consistent, and determined to discipline. If you don't, your children will suffer. This is one of my least favorite parts of parenting, but I love my kids too much not to do it.

BASIC RULES

Discipline is the area of parenting that triggers more emotion, defensiveness, and reactivity than any other. Even as a psychologist, I must tread carefully when speaking to parents about their discipline style. The first point to remember is that discipline is different from punishment. Discipline trains a child to do things better in the future. Punishment focuses on inflicting penalties for past performance. Discipline comes from an attitude of concern, and it ultimately builds respect and security in a child. Punishment usually comes from frustration or anger, and it tends to build fear or guilt in a child.

When applying discipline, both parents need to present a common front and agree on the discipline plan. When parents disagree (and they will disagree), they need to resolve these issues privately. It is incredibly confusing to children when they see that their mom and dad have different expectations for them. In fact, most children will try to take advantage of this situation, thus putting the child in a position of power that is not good for her or the family. So support your spouse in front of your child, even if you disagree with his or her style. Of course, there are a few key exceptions:

- physical or sexual abuse

- physical danger

- illegal activity

- immoral behavior

There are two special situations that are a bit more complicated. If you are a single parent, find a support person to help you brainstorm your discipline plan and back up the limits you set in place. If you are in a blended family, biological parents should do the majority of parenting for their children—unless the children were very young when you were married, the biological parent is often absent, or the child's behavior is out of control.

Now let's get down to the basic rules for healthy discipline:

1. Make rules age appropriate.
2. Explain limits and boundaries.
3. Focus on only three to five rules at a time.
4. Write down rules and post them.
5. Connect each rule with a consequence.
6. Avoid consequences you won't or can't enforce.
7. Be consistent, even when you're busy or tired.
8. Respond quickly with consequences.
9. Never discipline when you're angry.
10. Don't discipline for mistakes or accidents.
11. Follow through regardless of whining, crying, yelling, or tantrums.
12. Tell your children you love them.
13. Encourage them to do better next time.
14. Move on to something positive.

These rules will get you started, but before you go too far you need to consider what consequences you feel most comfortable with and which ones are most effective for your child.

BASIC CONSEQUENCES

The greatest problem of today's teenagers is not drugs, alcohol, sex, violence, peer pressure, defiance, depression, loneliness, disrespect, or laziness. It is the failure to understand that everything we do has a consequence. Each of the problems above has consequences or is the consequence of something else. If our children fail to understand the concept of consequences, they will struggle throughout life. Whenever I am driving somewhere with my kids, I love to play the "what if" game.

- What if I didn't stop at the next red light?

- What if we didn't eat for forty days?

- What if you robbed a bank?

This provides a fun way to help your child think about consequences.

Discipline requires some form of consequence if it's going to have any real meaning. If there are no powerful consequences, kids won't take the discipline seriously. Healthy consequences need to be *related* to the misbehavior. They must also be *reasonable* for the child's age and maturity. Without being abusive, they must be *rigorous* enough to get their attention. Lastly, they need to be *respectful* in that they don't shame or embarrass the offender. I've compiled ten of the most popular consequences for misbehavior below:

① Say no.
② Give a verbal reprimand.
③ Ignore them.
④ Walk away.

⑤ Allow natural consequences.

⑥ Implement a time-out.

⑦ Remove privileges, objects, or allowance.

⑧ Assign special tasks or additional chores.

⑨ Impose physical exercise (e.g., running, push-ups, etc.).

⑩ Deliver swats.

A chapter could easily be written on each one of these consequences. But since delivering swats is the most controversial yet one of the most popular forms of consequences, let me address this for a moment. The two greatest concerns with swats are that they can model aggressive behavior and they can cause physical harm. These are valid concerns, but if this is a form of consequence you feel comfortable with, there are simple guidelines that resolve these concerns.

- Never swat in anger.

- Avoid using swats on children younger than eighteen months and older than eleven years.

- Only swat on a child's behind or hand.

- Use swats as a last resort, after other techniques have failed.

- Explain the offense before you swat.

- Don't swat more than three times (even if the child doesn't cry).

- Swatting should be reserved for deliberate misbehavior or defiance.

- Only a parent or someone the parent trusts highly should swat.

- Administer swats privately.

- Never cause physical injury or marks.

- Both parents should agree on the use of swats.

- Embrace your child and show her love after a swat.

Consequences don't have to be negative. So far in this chapter we've looked at discipline that results from misbehavior. But don't focus solely on what your kids have done wrong. They do a lot right, and these things need to be rewarded with positive consequences. Research has shown that people learn faster when positive behavior is rewarded than when negative behavior is disciplined. As parents we need to be ready and willing to use both types of consequences.

IS IT FAIR?

Last night I was laughing and chatting with Dusty as he was getting ready for bed. It had been a good day, and he had worked hard with me. As he sat on his bed he said, "Dad, I don't think yesterday was fair."

"You mean when I disciplined you by saying you owed me six free lawn mowings because you had disobeyed your mother?"

"Yes," Dusty said. "I think six is too much."

"But you were being rude to your mother and me after we had just done something special for you. Why did you act like that?"

"I don't know," he said. "I'm sorry, and I think I should owe you one free lawn mowing, but six seems like too much."

"Maybe you're right," I said. "Let me think about it."

"Dad, isn't the purpose of discipline for me to learn a lesson?"

"Yes," I answered cautiously.

"I think one free lawn mowing will teach me the lesson."

"Maybe I was too hard on you yesterday. Let's try just one free lawn mowing for now, but if you don't learn your lesson you'll owe me the other five. Does that seem fair?"

"Yes." Dusty's smile covered his whole face. "That seems really fair."

TODAY'S TOOLS

Prayer

Dear God,

Teach me to discipline out of love, not out of anger, frustration, or fear. Help me to not be too quick or too slow to discipline.

Show me how to discipline in a positive way that teaches valuable lessons and encourages good behavior.

Empower me to discipline calmly, fairly, and firmly at the moment it is needed.

Energize me so I won't avoid or overlook discipline because I am tired, fearful, or lazy.

Direct me to the best way to discipline my children—considering their personalities, my temperament, and the situation.

Let my children know that I discipline them because I love them. If I discipline unfairly, give me the courage and humility to apologize and correct my mistake.

Let my children know that my love is not based on their good behavior. I love them even when they've just been disciplined.

Amen.

Passage

He who loves [his child] is careful to discipline him.
Proverbs 13:24

Practice

1. Write down five basic rules for your house and the consequences for breaking them. Review these rules with your kids, then post them somewhere they can be easily seen.
2. Talk to your spouse or a good friend about what discipline styles you feel most comfortable with and least comfortable with. Also discuss:

   what discipline is most appropriate for what age

   what discipline is most appropriate for what offense

   what discipline is most appropriate for what personality

3. Get together as a family and play the "what if" game. Ask questions that make your children think about consequences, such as:

   What if you started the house on fire?

   What if we didn't have a car?

   What if you broke the TV?

RULE ❾
PROVIDE A GREAT EXAMPLE

RAISING KIDS IS NOT EASY.

Parenting is hard work and it takes an enormous amount of patience. Your job is to bring your children from a point of immaturity to a point of maturity. It is to shape, mold, encourage, teach, train, love, guide, discipline, and direct them until they are healthy, responsible adults. A parent holds the most powerful and important job in the world.

I once heard the story about a very respected professor who had a PhD and three master's degrees. This man was so brilliant that he taught teachers how to be better teachers at a prestigious university. One day he was offered the position of president of this university. He carefully considered all the advantages and disadvantages of this generous offer before graciously declining it. In fact, he also resigned his teaching position. His colleagues were shocked.

"Why are you resigning?" they asked. "What are you going to do?"

"As I have evaluated how I might have the greatest impact on future generations," the respected professor said, "I have decided to teach kindergarten."

His colleagues stared in disbelief. "Kindergarten?"

"Think of it this way," he said. "Can you have more impact on dry cement or wet cement?"

Your child is wet cement.

When we built our house, some teenagers snuck into our garage and wrote their initials on the floor of the recently poured cement. Fifteen years later, the initials are still there. Marks on wet cement last a lifetime, so parents must be careful what they write.

When you are working with the wet cement of your child's heart, anything you do or say has the potential of leaving a mark. Your children are constantly watching and listening to you, even when you are totally unaware of it. At some level you are shaping their image of God, marriage, people, the world, and even themselves. Your kids are deeply affected by your words, but they are more influenced by what you do. While parents need to be aware that all they do influences their kids, certain areas need special focus.

GRACE AND ACCEPTANCE

Grace involves giving people a break when they make mistakes, do foolish things, or act imperfectly. Your kids watch how you treat other people and listen to what you say about them. If you are judgmental, demeaning, or demanding, your kids will follow your example. Everybody makes mistakes, does foolish things, and acts imperfectly, including your kids. If they see you rejecting others, they will wonder when you will reject them.

Acceptance involves trying to understand differences. Loving people means that you accept how they think and act and dress, even if it is not how you think, act, or dress. We live in a world that loves to divide everything into right or wrong. This usually means, *I'm right, you're wrong*.

Of course, I believe there are certain absolutes and it is very important that these are defended. Yet most of what people argue and debate about are simply preferences, opinions, and traditions. You can model acceptance and respect by fairly considering the pros and cons of *every* position, even your own. The best place to start showing grace and acceptance is toward your children. Let them know your acceptance by telling them things such as:

- "You are one of a kind, unique, special, significant."

- "I would not trade you for anyone in this world."

- "I love you because you are you."

- "I appreciate you."

- "There is no one else who could ever take your place."

When grace is not present, it leaves its marks of pain, insecurity, inadequacy, and rejection. Actor Sylvester Stallone acknowledged the scars he experienced when he wrote, "My father was an extraordinarily exacting man, and if what you did wasn't a photocopy of the way he did it, then you had no abilities and had to be chastised and corrected. He made me feel extraordinarily inept. Why can't you be smarter? Why can't you be stronger? I didn't have one virtue. He never said he was proud of me." His father missed an opportunity to model grace and acceptance.

CHARACTER

Kids need to see their parents doing the right thing.

Dylan was seven, and we were at the local grocery store. The cashier rang up our food and handed me the change. As we walked out of the store I said, "I think she gave me too much change." I stopped and quickly recounted it. Yes, she had given me a dollar too much.

"Dylan, what should we do?" I asked.

"Give the dollar back," he said without hesitation.

So the two of us returned to the cashier. "Excuse me," I said, "but you gave me a dollar too much in change."

She stared at me with a look of disbelief.

"I just want to give you back a dollar," I said, and handed back the money.

She took the dollar bill and turned to Dylan. "You should be proud of your father, because he is an honest man."

I hadn't done anything great. I just did the right thing when I didn't have to. That's what character is all about.

Character is passed on by example more than by any other method. It takes work to pass on good character, but bad character gets passed on naturally with little effort.

- If you are impatient, your children will struggle with impatience.

- If you lie, your children will struggle with lying.

- If you are unfaithful, your children will struggle with unfaithfulness.

Therefore, be careful what you do, because it will get passed on to your children. Living with someone of a positive character is a heritage your children will never forget. Will Rogers Jr. once said the following words about his father: "His heritage to his children wasn't words or possessions, but an unspoken treasure, the treasure of his example as a man and a father. More than anything I have, I'm trying to pass that on to my children." Will's father passed on character to his children—a true treasure.

DELAYED GRATIFICATION

In this materialistic, I-want-it-now culture, parents need to model that you don't need everything you want and you don't need it immediately. There is value in saving up for something and waiting to get it. Immediate gratification feeds materialism. When we get something too easily or quickly, we don't value it as much as we would if we had to work and wait for it. New things are fun and exciting, but they lose their appeal quickly, leaving us looking for the next new thing. Kids who get a lot expect a lot. When kids are given too much too soon, they grow up to be adults who are easily disappointed when things don't go their way.

Show your children what patience looks like by avoiding impulsive spending. If there is something you want, talk about it and plan for it. Don't just run out and get it. It's good to show your kids that they can't have everything, that sometimes they have to be patient and make choices. It's tempting to compare what you have to what others have, but if you model contentedness, your kids will learn to be content. There is a good reason that the tenth commandment says, "You shall not covet" (Exodus 20:17).

Delayed gratification helps minimize materialism. Here are a few more ways to teach this to your kids:

- Show that you can have fun without spending money.

- Remind them that people matter more than things.

- Encourage your children to save, recycle, reuse, share, give away, and take care of things you have.

- Model debt-free living.

- Discuss the living conditions in third world countries and of those who have less than your family.

- Say "No," "Not yet," and "We don't need that."

- Thank God for all that you have.

- Avoid having to have the newest, the best, or the most of anything.

I know this goes against our cultural pattern, but it's a lesson your children will cherish for the rest of their lives.

OPTIMISM

Negativity is contagious; it is like a drop of black ink in a jar of clear water. Within a few minutes the whole jar is murky and contaminated. Yet with a positive attitude, you can teach your children to rise above frustration, unhappiness, and anger. When I think of optimism, I think of the following four characteristics.

Being able to laugh: A good sense of humor can lighten the most tense situation. Children need to see that you can have fun and be joyful. Laughter makes everything a little better.

Looking for positives: We are surrounded by positives, but sometimes we have to look for them. If we look for negatives, we'll find them. Yet focusing on the positives is like standing in the sunshine.

Giving compliments: When your kids see you encouraging and building others up, they learn a powerful skill. Compliments can make you feel better about someone and help that person to feel better about you.

Counting your blessings: Learning to be thankful and expressing thankfulness reminds you that things are frequently better than you think. When your children see you being grateful, they will begin to appreciate all they have as well.

Optimism can be learned, and it's best learned when children see it in their parents.

RELATIONSHIPS

Kids need to see their parents building healthy relationships with others. Much of life involves social situations in which people must interact with each other. When your children see you connecting with neighbors, relatives, friends, acquaintances, and strangers, they develop social skills of their own. Your kids need to see you:

- helping others

- inviting people to your home

- encouraging others

- having fun with people

- working alongside others

- sharing meals together

- problem solving with others

- talking through issues

- respecting differences in others

- doing ministry side by side

As parents, not only do we need to bond with others, we also need to bond with our kids. Reaching out to your kids—talking with them, playing with them, helping them, laughing with them—builds a foundation from which your children can feel secure enough to reach out and connect with their peers.

Jack and his ten-year-old son, Jason, had a great connection. So when Jason developed cancer and went through chemotherapy, Jack saw how alone his son felt. Without hesitation, Jack shaved off his thick, wavy brown hair. Jason was so excited that his father would go so far as to shave his own head just so the two of them would look the same. Jason never forgot that lesson; it taught him to reach out to those who feel isolated or alienated.

FAITH

Faith is the most important gift you can give your child. I once had a college professor who was an avid atheist. One day the class was discussing the scheduling of a field trip. Someone suggested Sunday as the best day. "I'm sorry," the professor said, "but Sundays won't work. That's the day I take my children to church."

Curiosity got the better of me, so I asked, "Why would someone who doesn't believe in God take his children to church?"

"Because I love my kids and take parenting seriously," was the response. "There aren't a lot of places in our culture that teach healthy values. Church is one of those places."

Even people with little or no faith see its value. Faith gives your child purpose and direction. It provides a value system and a sense of peace when difficulties crash down upon them. Corrie ten Boom writes that "faith is like radar that sees through the fog." There certainly is a lot of fog in this world, and our children need a way to see through it. Faith becomes that way.

Your children need your help in finding their faith. They need to see you practicing, discussing, and living a godly life. They need to see you praying, attending church, seeking forgiveness, helping the poor, reading Scripture, seeking God's presence, resting in God, and exploring spiritual issues. They need to see your faith incorporated into your daily life, for when they see it is real to you it can become real to them.

Faith has many facets that help a child grasp the nature and person of God. Some of these faith-building opportunities are:

① seeking God
② knowing God
③ communicating with God
④ embracing God
⑤ loving God

⑥ following God

⑦ serving God

⑧ reflecting God

As parents, we have incredible power to influence and encourage our children's faith through these eight ways. Yet through passivity, inconsistency, or compromise, we may also confuse or discourage our children to such an extent that they reject or lose their faith.

POINT THE WAY

Children need an example to follow. They need to see you modeling what a healthy spouse, parent, friend, neighbor, adult, and Christian looks like. If you don't set a positive example, there are plenty of people who will set a negative one for your kids. Your children are too precious to risk letting peers or strangers show them the way. Karyn Henley writes in *Child-Sensitive Teaching*, "Children are natural seekers; they just need us to point the way." After all, isn't that our job?

TODAY'S TOOLS

Prayer

Dear God,

Forgive me for all the times I have been a poor example, showing my children what they should not do. Strengthen me as I try to model for them what is healthy, wise, positive, good, and right.

Build in me an example of grace and acceptance, so my children will learn how to not be judgmental.

Build in me an example of character, so my children will learn how to show integrity.

Build in me an example of delayed gratification, so my children will learn how to be patient.

Build in me an example of optimism, so my children will learn how to be content, regardless of their circumstances.

Build in me an example of healthy relationships, so my children will learn how to genuinely love.

Build in me an example of faith, so my children will learn how to daily walk with God.

Thank you for providing us the ultimate example of all these things in your beloved Son.

Amen.

Passage

In everything set them an example by doing what is good.
Titus 2:7

Practice

① Come up with five practical examples of how you or your family could demonstrate grace and acceptance.

② Gather as a family to discuss people, living or dead, who serve as powerful examples of:

a person of character

a person of optimism

a person of faith

③ Ask each member of your family to choose someone for whom they can do an anonymous good deed. Arrange a meeting in one week to discuss what you did and how it turned out.

RULE ❿
TELL THEM YOU LOVE THEM

"LET'S GO DRIVING!" Dylan said with excitement.

I had a hundred things to do, but my fifteen-year-old had just gotten his driver's permit and wanted to practice his skills. After a moment's hesitation I said, "Why don't you ask your mother?"

"I already asked her," Dylan said. "She says that teaching us to drive is your job."

"Okay," I said. "Let's go!"

After an hour of driving every back road around our house, Dylan and I drove to McDonald's to get milk shakes. As we sat in the car having a great time I said, "Now remind me why I am spending my afternoon teaching you to drive."

"Because you love me," he said with a smile.

He was absolutely right.

Kids need to know that you love them, and they need to be reminded of it frequently. If we focus too much on the ways our kids frustrate us, they'll start to believe that we wish we had other children instead of them. Too often we are better at communicating the negative than the positive. We believe it is so obvious we love our kids that we don't bother to say it. Here are a few ways to say you love them.

USE YOUR WORDS

The best way to communicate love is with direct, no-question-about-it bluntness. You simply say, "I love you." Then you repeat it over and over until the message is so embedded in their memories that they can't forget it. Every day I tell my kids I love them—when they're good, when they frustrate me, when they disobey, when they are successful, when they fail. I want them to know that my love is unconditional. Say it strongly. Say it frequently. Say it consistently.

Dusty and I have a little game we play. I ask, "Who loves you?" and he says, "You do!"

"How do you know that?"

He sighs and says something like, "Because you tell me all the time."

I don't believe you can ever say "I love you" too much, but there are other ways to communicate love. One of my favorites is through compliments. Compliments encourage us, making us feel better about ourselves as well as the one who gave them. Consider the following seven types of compliments that tell your kids you love them.

① Appearance: Let them know that they look good.
② Attitude: Tell them you are proud of how they're handling a situation.
③ Accomplishments: Emphasize things that they have done well.
④ Attempts: Reassure them that giving their best effort is impressive.
⑤ Abilities: Recognize their strengths, talents, and skills.

⑥ Actions: Praise them for positive, compassionate, and good deeds.

⑦ Attributes: Spotlight their virtues and admirable character traits.

Each of these types of compliments communicates clearly that you love your kids.

If you can't say it in person, do it in writing. Cards and notes are wonderful ways to say "I love you" or pass on a compliment. Some people communicate better through writing. It may not be as personal as saying something face-to-face, but it has the advantage of permanence. The words you write to your children can be read and reread years after they were written. You don't have to be a smooth or eloquent writer. You don't even have to spell correctly or use proper grammar. All you have to do is share your heart; your kids will get the message. So I encourage you to deliver your words any way you can. Speak them one day and write them the next. Words are powerful and will give your children hope when they feel lonely, defeated, or discouraged.

BE GENEROUS

There are hundreds of small, daily ways to generously show love to your kids. Be generous with your respect. Show kindness and patience. Be gentle with them and treat them with the same politeness you would show a friend. Let them know you think positively of them. Stand by them as people, even if you disagree with their behavior. Respect doesn't mean you agree or approve of their actions. It also doesn't mean that they won't have to face difficult or uncomfortable consequences.

What it does mean is that you will love them in spite of their failures or foolishness.

Be generous with your affection. I love to hug my kids. Giving your kids appropriate physical contact is a powerful way of communicating love. When they are younger, you can kiss them or hold their hands. As they grow older, you can put your arm around their shoulders or pat their backs. Physical contact is a source of security, safety, and comfort. This is important to every kid, regardless of age. Yet some children seem to crave this type of contact more than others. Dusty's love language is physical touch. If you scratch his back, he thinks you are his best friend.

Sometimes generosity is best shown through presents. Giving your child something tangible makes your love seem more real and solid. I still have certain gifts my parents gave me when I was a child. These are treasures to me. These presents have an emotional value that is priceless. Each of these gifts is a symbol of my parents' love for me. Gifts don't have to be big or expensive to be meaningful. Sometimes the best gifts are the simplest and the smallest. I enjoy giving things to my kids. I want them to have tangible symbols of my love for them, whether it's earrings for Brittany, a pocketknife for Dylan, or one of my classic watches for Dusty. Each of these is given from a heart of love.

Sometimes what your child needs more than anything else is a little help. Of course, there is a big difference between a little help and too much help. Often out of frustration and impatience, parents move in and take over a project. After all, in many situations we can do whatever needs to be done faster and better than our children. Yet when you do this, you frequently send the wrong message. Inadvertently your actions might communicate:

- "You are too slow."

- "You can't do anything right."

- "If you are going to do something, you have to do it my way."

- "You are stupid."

To avoid these implications, either wait until they ask and then work alongside them or ask them directly if they would like some help. As you assist them you may make suggestions, but don't take over the project or insist that they do it your way. Remember, you are the project assistant, not the project manager.

It was about six o'clock on a Sunday night when Dylan came to Tami and me with a worried look on his face. "I think I'm stuck."

As the conversation unfolded, we discovered he had a major project due the next day that was only partially completed. The more he told us about what he was trying to do, the more we realized he didn't have enough time to complete it by himself.

"Dylan, would you like some help?" I asked.

"Sure," he said, as his face immediately brightened.

During the next four hours, everybody in our family came alongside Dylan to help him complete his project. It was a fun evening, but more important, we showed Dylan that we loved him enough to set aside our activities and help him with his.

Another way to say "I love you" is by being generous with your time. This involves crawling into your children's world and connecting with them at their level. This might mean sharing an activity, a hobby, an interest, a sport, a trip, a project, or even a conversation. As you discover your children's interests, spend time exploring those interests with them. I talk about psychology and watch movies with Brittany. I go to concerts and read books with Dylan. I cheer at soccer games and go treasure hunting at Goodwill with Dusty. One of the best ways to give your love as a parent is to get involved in their world.

NEVER TOO MUCH

People often ask me if it's possible to love our kids too much. My answer is always the same: "Absolutely not." However, it's important to understand what love is. Love is doing what is best for our kids over the long haul. It is investing in them so that they can be as physically, emotionally, mentally, socially, and spiritually healthy as possible. Love is not:

- smothering them

- spoiling them

- doing everything their way

- protecting them from consequences

- refusing to discipline them

- tolerating inappropriate behavior

Your children will first learn love from you, and your love is the most important love they will ever experience. It can't be replaced by anyone else. So express your love often. Say it with words that will echo in their hearts the rest of their lives. Say it with generosity—giving them respect, physical contact, presents, help, and quality time. Love is more powerful than most of us ever realize.

TODAY'S TOOLS

Prayer

Dear God,

Sometimes I don't want to love. Maybe I'm too tired or too frustrated or too busy. Sometimes I'm not in the mood or have better things to do. Yet you always love me, even when I don't deserve it.

Thank you for always being there.

Help me to love my children as consistently and unconditionally as you love me.

Help me to tell them directly, in their face.

Help me to tell them through sincere compliments.

Help me to tell them through hugs, presents, help, and quality time.

Never let me forget the amazing power of love. Fill me with your love so that I can spread it generously to all I come in contact with. Let me give a triple portion to my spouse and children.

Amen.

Passage

Live a life of love.
Ephesians 5:2

Practice

(1) Say "I love you" to each one of your children every day for the next two weeks.

(2) Write down seven compliments for each of your children—one compliment for each of the following a's:

> *appearance*
>
> *attitude*
>
> *accomplishments*
>
> *attempts*
>
> *abilities*
>
> *actions*
>
> *attributes*

(3) Find an inexpensive, meaningful gift to give each of your children as a symbol of how much you love them.

RULE ⓫
CHOOSE YOUR BATTLES

"CUT YOUR HAIR."

"Don't waste your money on that."

"If you don't eat everything on your plate, you're grounded."

"Do it this way or you're in trouble."

"Don't touch that."

Parenting is full of battles. Some are important to fight; some aren't. If you try to fight every battle that comes your way, you will burn yourself out and frustrate your children. They will give up, feeling that they can't do anything right. And when your kids give up, they will go in one of the following directions:

- They will agree to your face, while doing whatever they want behind your back.

- They will defy you, since they think that no matter what they do they can't make you happy.

- They will wait for their freedom, then they'll do all that they can to prove that you can't control them anymore.

Neither empty compliance nor angry defiance will accomplish what you want as a parent. Setting boundaries is necessary in every family, but there must be a balance. Too many boundaries can be overcontrolling, while too few lead to irresponsibility. To find the balance, you must choose your battles: Figure out when to let go, when to negotiate, and when to stand firm.

LETTING GO

Sometimes I can be a control freak. I like everything neat and in order. Before we had kids, everything *was* tidy and in its place. Yet once we had kids, our household changed. Things got messy; life got messy. Nothing ever seemed to be as neat as I thought it should be. My expectations were disappointed daily. For a while I held tightly to my fantasy of everything being in perfect order. In the process, I drove Tami nuts and made my children uptight. Ultimately, I had to face the fact that everything can't be perfect. As I let go of this, I was happier and so was everybody else in my family.

Letting go is sometimes the wisest thing a parent can do. A lot of issues are trivial and not that important in the big picture. As my grandmother used to say, "What difference will it make in five years?" Your children are unique individuals. As they go through the stages of growing up, you will find that at times they appear to be very similar to you. Yet at other times you will be shocked, frustrated, and maybe even perplexed at how different they can be. Don't panic. This is just part of parenting.

Your kids will not be carbon copies of you. Their preferences and opinions will sometimes be different. If you force them to conform on every issue, you had better be prepared for a lot of conflict. As your kids grow older, they will need to define themselves as unique individuals. They will experiment with things such as:

- different clothes
- different hobbies
- different music
- different hair
- different jewelry styles
- different ideas about spending money
- different sense of order
- different ways to do things

Differences aren't bad, but sometimes they will frustrate you, frighten you, or cause you to scratch your head in confusion. Yet every generation has to create its own unique personality.

Elizabeth's sixteen-year-old son, Michael, was tearing the family apart. Michael wouldn't talk to his dad, and his dad wouldn't talk to him. Elizabeth tried to be the peacemaker, but now both her son and her husband were upset at her for taking the other's side. Michael was a handsome teenager with a shaved head. He said he liked it because it set him apart from the crowd. His father hated Michael's drastic haircut and demanded that he let it grow. Michael's father was also handsome, but in contrast, he had long, shoulder-length locks. Both were trying to make statements about individuality using their hairstyles.

Instead of fighting, I encouraged Michael's father to let go and love his son. He agreed that this was a foolish fight. So instead of arguing about hair length, Michael's father decided to focus on something more productive: snowboarding! Now their biggest battles occur on the slopes, as they challenge each other and race to the bottom.

NEGOTIATE

Ted hates the word *negotiate*.

"Why should I have to negotiate with my kids?" he asked me. "I should be able to tell them what to do, and they should just do it. What's wrong with that?"

"There are times when kids need to just obey," I told him. "But there are other times when negotiating is a wonderful opportunity to connect with your kids."

Negotiation can have great benefits for both parents and kids.

- It encourages communication skills.

- It teaches kids how to work with adults.

- It helps us learn how to make decisions and compromises.

- It shows respect.

- It allows us to understand someone else's perspective.

- It focuses on responsibilities and priorities.

At its core, negotiation is all about problem solving and communication. I want my kids to know that I'm willing to talk about anything.

Even if I say no to a request, I want them to know that they can ask, "Why?" My kids have also learned to ask, "Is that 'no' negotiable or nonnegotiable?" Sometimes if my children can address my concerns, I'm willing to change my mind. But even if they can't get me to change my mind, I'm still willing to discuss the issue with them. They might not like my decision or even agree with it, but I want them to understand why I made it. Unhealthy families have a "never question my authority" rule. This shuts down communication and thus shuts down understanding.

How you parent your children changes with their age and maturity. The things you are willing to negotiate when they are fourteen will be different from when they were four. Also, as your kids get older, it's important that you be willing to negotiate more and more issues. This is called *developmental parenting*. When kids are young, parents take the role of teacher, provider, and protector. As your kids move into adolescence, you transition into being their encourager, supporter, and facilitator. Then when they are adults, you become their friend, companion, and colleague. If you refuse to change your role as your kids grow up, they will either rebel or remain emotionally immature.

There are a lot of things I'm willing to negotiate about with my kids. I'll negotiate bedtime, vacations, clothing, purchases, and special privileges, to name just a few. Yet as we negotiate, I try to teach them healthy priorities. Certain things in life are more important than other things. Some of the priorities I want to teach my kids fall into the following order:

① God
② parents

③ family
④ school
⑤ extracurricular activities and friends

When I teach children how to negotiate with their parents, I try to get them to follow these steps:

① Think through what you want and how important it is to you.
② Consider why your parents might not be supportive of your request.
③ Check your attitude to make sure it is not demanding, demeaning, or defiant.
④ Share your request politely and clearly.
⑤ Explain why this is important to you.
⑥ Express what you think your parents' concerns might be.
⑦ Provide possible solutions to their concerns.
⑧ Listen to your parents' responses without interruption.
⑨ Discuss the situation calmly.
⑩ Defer to your parents.

I tell most kids this: When you rationally and respectfully discuss issues, you are more likely to get what you want. It won't work every time, but it will work more often than any other strategy I know.

Timing can be everything. Negotiations sometimes derail because of bad timing. So the big question is, "When is a good time?" When the negotiations are one-on-one, make plans to go for a drive or take a walk or visit a restaurant. Yet when negotiations affect the entire family, plan a family meeting. I can almost hear the universal groan of "Oh no." But stop for a minute. Family meetings can be positive, exciting, and a lot of fun. Here are some rules to help you get started:

① Try to make family meetings a regular event.
② Allow any family member to call a family meeting.
③ Don't leave anyone out; all family members must be present.
④ Turn off televisions, CD players, cell phones, and any other distractions.
⑤ Each person has the opportunity to express his or her feelings and set the topic.
⑥ Be polite—no one has the right to dominate, insult, abuse, embarrass, or manipulate other family members.
⑦ Only discuss one topic at a time, and try to resolve one issue before moving on to the next.
⑧ Take notes to make sure there are no questions about what is decided.
⑨ Allow the kids to be a part of planning and decisions, but explain that parents always have the final say.
⑩ Keep meetings brief and fun.

Follow your family meeting with something special, such as a movie, a sporting event, a chocolate cake, a bike ride, or something else that every family member will enjoy.

STAND FIRM

In every family some things are nonnegotiable. You can't burn down the house. You can't rob the local bank. You can't amputate your sister's little finger. These things are not acceptable. Parents cannot let go of or negotiate these issues. These are areas that are important enough that you are willing to do battle over them. They need to be thought through, and your kids need to understand your determination about them. My own five nonnegotiables involve things that are:

- immoral

- illegal

- unsafe

- unhealthy

- cruel

There are two other areas that some parents also include: things that are rude and things that are unwise. These are important areas, but I wanted my list to be as short as possible. I also knew that these areas are difficult to define and enforce at times. Yet I certainly don't want my kids to do rude or unwise things.

When parents stand firm, they don't budge. They explain the principle behind their stand without getting angry or belittling their kids. They speak the truth in love, letting their children know that they are not trying to limit or squash them. Love needs limits, and there are times these limits must stand firm, regardless of the pressure. Many parents tell me that standing firm is one of the toughest parts of parenting. I know it's tough, but it's crucial. My only warning is to make sure you are standing firm on only the most important issues. Choose your battles, but when you must battle, do it with all the love and determination you can muster.

CHOOSE WISELY

My parents had six active, independent, and sometimes stubborn children. If they had tried to fight every battle, they'd have burned out very quickly. They chose not to say anything about how long I grew my hair, but they would frequently ground me from a particular friend who made poor choices. They were quiet about what music I listened to, but they watched my grades carefully. My parents chose their battles. We kids might not have agreed with our parents, but we respected them. Thirty years later, all six of us are successful adults with healthy marriages and great families. We aren't perfect. We make mistakes. But Mom and Dad taught us certain values and skills with which to live life. I think one of the most important lessons was to choose your battles.

TODAY'S TOOLS

Prayer

Dear God,

Parenting is sometimes confusing. It is not always clear how best to handle difficult situations. Yet you are the source of all wisdom, with answers to my every question.

Show me when to let go so I will not create battles over issues that are secondary or irrelevant in the big picture.

Teach me when to negotiate in a calm, meaningful way so I can communicate principles and help my kids think through challenging situations.

Strengthen me when I need to stand firm so I can help my kids understand that there are certain issues that are so important they must be fought for.

Remind me that part of my job as a parent is to protect and educate my children. Assist me in doing this in a loving way that helps them to grow into wise, healthy, and compassionate adults.

Amen.

Passage

If any of you lacks wisdom, he should ask God, who gives generously to all without finding fault, and it will be given to him.

James 1:5

Practice

1. Sit down with your spouse or a good friend and discuss which battles are worth the fight.
2. Set up a date for a family meeting. Bake cookies or have some special treat when the time arrives. Make it fun and positive. Encourage everybody to interact about the following questions:

   What is something that happened recently that didn't seem fair?

   What is a family rule you would like to get rid of?

   What is a new family rule you would like to put in place?

   What is something fun you would like to do in the next three months?

3. Make a list of five items that you believe you need to stand firm on as a parent.

RULE ⑫
MAKE YOUR MARRIAGE GREAT

I LOVE TO KISS MY WIFE.

One night I came home later than usual. I walked into the kitchen, wrapped my arms around Tami, and gave her a great big kiss. All three kids reacted with comments like, "Yuck," "Don't do that," and "Stop that right now!" Maybe there is a rebellious teenager hidden deep in my heart, because the more they protested, the more I wanted to kiss Tami. Soon the kids were trying to tear us apart, so Tami and I stopped kissing each other and started kissing them. The kids tried to run away, but we chased them down. Together we hugged and kissed and laughed until our sides ached.

Your kids need to see you kiss. They might protest and complain, but inside they are telling themselves, *Everything is okay with Mom and Dad, so everything is okay with me.*

My daughter insists, "It is gross when people over thirty kiss."

I laugh and reply, "But your mom is such a good kisser."

Brittany gives me a dirty look and walks away, but not before I catch a glimpse of that little smile she's trying to hide. All kids want to know that Mom and Dad love each other. As parents, you are the foundation of the family. When the marriage is stable, so is the family. This doesn't mean that you have to have the perfect marriage. In fact, the perfect marriage doesn't exist. Every couple fights and disagrees, gets angry and disappointed, has hard times, and says things they regret. Yet marriage, regardless of its flaws, is the healthiest place to raise children (unless there is physical, sexual, or extreme emotional abuse). After working with families for more than twenty-five years, I have concluded that the best gift we can give our children is a great marriage.

WHY DIVORCE DOESN'T WORK

Weddings are a time of celebration, while divorces are a tragedy. Sometimes divorce is necessary, but it should be the painful exception, not the rule. Divorce is a serious decision that should be approached thoughtfully, prayerfully, and with a great deal of wise counsel. Other than a handful of exceptions noted in Scripture, divorce is never a good alternative.

Divorce is an attempt to solve a problem: boredom, betrayal, loss of love, hurt, loneliness, insecurity, hopelessness, fear, abuse, or neglect. Yet most of the time ending a marriage simply exchanges one set of problems for another set of equally painful problems. Most people are better off staying married and putting their time, energy, and money into improving what they have, rather than trying to start over somewhere else. Unfortunately, some individuals don't have a choice, and they become victims of divorce. Yet the bottom line is this: Except for a few specific and tragic situations, divorce doesn't work. Consider this:

(1) Divorce rarely solves the problem. Difficulties in a marriage usually involve both parties; rather than blaming your spouse, work on fixing yourself.

② Divorce is a financial disaster. Divorce is not cheap, and starting over is expensive, since two households cost more than one.

③ Divorce blocks personal growth. Maturity comes from working through your problems with patience and determination, not running away from them.

④ Divorce sets you up for repetition. Most people carry their problems into the next relationship, repeating the same mistakes they've previously made.

⑤ Divorce hardens your heart. Divorce can escalate negative emotions, making you self-protective, hard, and less sensitive to God and others.

⑥ Divorce hurts friends and relatives. Those who love you are left confused and frustrated as to whom to support and what to do.

⑦ Divorce affects your legacy. A failed relationship, along with all the people left in its wake, becomes part of your story.

⑧ Divorce disappoints God. Marriage is sacred, and though God is full of grace and mercy, he still hates divorce.

God hates divorce because he doesn't like to see people hurt. Divorce creates pain. You will hurt and your spouse will hurt, but the greatest victims will be your children.

WHAT ABOUT THE KIDS?

Three cute little girls, ages four to nine, sat politely in the large over-stuffed chairs in my office. Their parents were in the waiting room. My job was to see how the kids were dealing with the divorce.

"I'm curious," I said. "Why do you think your parents brought you here?"

"They're getting a divorce," said Jessie, the oldest of the three.

"Why do you think they are getting a divorce?"

"I don't know," said Jessie, "but I hate it."

"Me too," said Nicole.

"But you know they both love you very much," I said gently.

"If they loved us, they wouldn't do this," said Jessie.

"They're mean," added Nicole.

"Sometimes adults do things that don't make sense," I explained. "But your parents don't want to hurt you. In fact, they would do anything for you."

"Then why don't they stop getting divorced?" asked four-year-old Caitlyn. As tears fell from her little face, she said, "I want them to kiss and be nice so we can be a family again."

I was silent. I knew that nothing I could say would erase the pain these little girls were feeling.

Divorce hurts children more than most of us ever realize. Yes, children are resilient and there are ways parents can reduce the negative effects, but divorce leaves scars that linger for decades. In their classic work, *The Case for Marriage: Why Married People Are Happier, Healthier, and Better Off Financially*, Linda Waite and Maggie Gallagher conclude that most divorces leave children educationally, financially, and psychologically worse off. Researchers have found that divorce has the following impact on children:

- more academic struggles

- increased high school dropout rate

- more health problems

- more emotional problems (especially with anger, anxiety, loneliness, insecurity, and depression)

- increased risk of suicide

- increased likelihood of alcohol and drug abuse

- higher incidence of aggression and violence

- increased likelihood of run-ins with the law

- increased difficulty connecting with parents

- increased difficulty connecting with peers

- decreased self-confidence

- increased likelihood of sexual promiscuity

- increased likelihood of divorce in their own lives

- decreased life span

- higher probability of rejecting their parents' faith

I hate this list. I wish it weren't true, but this is reality, and it's something every parent must face.

Some of you might read this list and feel a knot in your stomach. You love your kids and you want the very best for them, but your marriage has fallen apart. This list is not to make you feel guilty or inadequate. The past is the past, and I just want to encourage you to do the best you can from this point forward. Single parents have a tough job, and I'm always amazed at what a great job they do. My prayers and admiration go to them.

If you are divorced, work with your ex-spouse as much as possible. Don't allow the kids to become pawns. Speak respectfully of your ex. Find something positive to say about him, even if it's hard. Your kids need to have a good relationship with both of you. You may no longer be husband and wife, but you will always be parents. Don't allow your hurts and frustrations to force your kids to choose between the two of you. Every child needs two parents—even if they live in separate houses.

If you are married, invest in making your marriage the best it can be. A great marriage is hard work, but it is worth it. You get out of a marriage what you are willing to put into it. I find that whatever I am willing to do to improve my marriage, Tami will match my effort twofold. Yet it is so easy to become selfish or lazy or distracted. Here are ten gifts to give each other that are guaranteed to enrich your relationship:

1. Communication: sharing your hopes, fears, and thoughts with each other
2. Laughter: playing and having fun together
3. Encouragement: looking for opportunities to compliment and build each other up
4. Comfort: providing love and care whenever needed
5. Flexibility: releasing your wishes and agenda to do it her way
6. Forgiveness: letting go of the past and refusing to bring it up again
7. Listening: focusing on one another's words and taking them seriously

⑧ Respect: treating each other with patience and understanding

⑨ Generosity: showing your love by giving time, words, gifts, and memories

⑩ Prayer: placing your marriage and spouse regularly in God's hands

Keeping your marriage healthy makes everybody a winner.

If your spouse has died or abandoned you, find a healthy support system. During times like these, your child needs you more than ever before, but parenting is a heavy burden for just one set of shoulders. Ask friends and relatives to come alongside you when you're feeling overwhelmed and alongside your children when they need a parental figure to fill the void left by loss.

GOING FOR THE LONG RUN

I love to hear how couples celebrate their wedding anniversaries. For our twentieth anniversary Tami and I went to Puerto Vallarta, Mexico. Some friends of ours went to a romantic bed-and-breakfast on the Oregon coast for their anniversary. Another couple went to a fancy resort in Hawaii, and still another went camping at a primitive site near a beautiful, secluded lake. Anniversaries are events that should be celebrated. They are wonderful statements of love, commitment, and survival.

Several years ago my brothers and sisters and I planned a celebration for my parents' fiftieth wedding anniversary. Fifty years—what an accomplishment! They deserved a celebration. The fact that my parents kept their wedding vows and stayed together has had a positive impact on all six of their children. Mom and Dad set an example of commitment for us to follow. Their marriage is not perfect, but we have always known that they care for each other. They provided a safe and secure environment in which we could grow up. We knew we were loved. We knew Mom and Dad were a team. We knew that even if they fought or disagreed, they would work it out. For over fifty years they have laughed and cried, worked and played, struggled and dreamed, but through it all they have done it together.

Thank you, Mom and Dad. Your togetherness has helped me be a better husband and parent and person.

TODAY'S TOOLS

Prayer

Dear God,

Forgive me for the times when marriage has been tough and I have not worked hard enough to make it better. Also forgive me for all the times I have not listened, been sensitive, or treasured my spouse. Forgive me for not being 100 percent committed to improving our relationship.

Place in my heart the passion I had in the early days of our marriage to honor and respect and encourage my beloved.

Teach us to listen and understand, laugh and play, comfort and forgive.

Teach us how to pray for each other—for our commitment, our oneness, our frustrations, our dreams, our faith—every single day.

Teach me to be more generous and less greedy, more sensitive and less selfish, more caring and less distracted.

Teach me how to show love to my spouse every morning, every evening, and every moment in between.

Amen.

Passage

Each one of you also must love his wife as he loves himself, and the wife must respect her husband.

Ephesians 5:33

Practice

① If you are single, find a friend, family member, neighbor, or person at church who would be willing to be an encourager and sounding board when you need to deal with parenting issues.

② If you are married, determine which of the following gifts you are best at and which you are worst at in terms of giving to your spouse:

communication

encouragement

forgiveness

respect

generosity

③ Make a commitment to read a book, watch a DVD, attend a seminar, or go to a retreat about strengthening your marriage at least once a year.

RULE ⓭
MORE BOOKS AND LESS TV

"WHY DO YOU READ SO MUCH?"

"Because it's fun," answered my father.

Fun? Why would anybody think reading is fun? When I was six years old, I could think of a hundred things that were fun, and reading was nowhere on my list.

My father was always reading something. Each morning it was the newspaper. In the evening it may have been a book on history or science fiction. Or maybe it was one of the many magazines that came in the mail: *Newsweek, U.S. News & World Report, Life, National Geographic,* or *Reader's Digest.* Sometimes when I was bored, I'd go into my father's library and just look at the books—hundreds and hundreds of them.

I didn't learn to read until I was eight, and I didn't understand my father's statement about fun until I was twelve. Then suddenly I got it. Books weren't just paper pages bound into little packages; they were doorways into the imagination that seemed to have no limit. Opening a volume in my father's library could transport me to prehistoric Europe or futuristic Mars and a thousand places in between. My mind reeled with possibilities as I embarked on adventures that seem as boundless and exciting now as they did nearly forty years ago.

Reading should be a family affair. It is best taught, encouraged, modeled, and reinforced in the family. I remember sitting on two-year-old Brittany's bed and asking her, "What would you like me to read tonight?"

"*Owl Moon*," was her enthusiastic reply.

"But we read that last night."

"*Owl Moon*," she said again, more emphatically.

So for the hundredth time, I read *Owl Moon*. We looked at each picture and talked about the story—the snow, the dark, the cold, and especially the owl. We had a great time. Somehow this story of a father and his daughter looking for owls brought us closer. Books can have a powerful impact on your family, if you give them a chance.

THE JOYS OF READING

Reading is one of the most important skills any person can learn. It is at the core of our educational system and paves the path to success in school and in life. Without basic reading skills, your child will struggle with everything from self-confidence to spiritual growth to career options. Reading is a gift that every parent can give his child. Bob Hostetler wrote that reading can:

- widen horizons

- stimulate imaginations

- counter the influence of television

- encourage the discovery of new interests

- strengthen family togetherness

- provide a storehouse of fond memories

I love to talk to my kids about what they're reading. It's fun to hear what they have learned or what happened in their books. Dusty has been reading about the Bermuda Triangle this past week, and each night he likes to share some interesting fact he's just discovered. Last weekend Dylan was reading in his Bible about the prophet Elijah, but something about the passage confused him. So he came to me and we had a wonderful talk about this amazing man. If it hadn't been for reading, I would have missed these opportunities to connect with my boys.

Fill your home with interesting reading materials—books, newspapers, magazines, pamphlets. Whenever my kids develop an interest in some new topic, we start exploring. First, we see if we have any books on the subject. If we don't, we go to the computer, the library, or the bookstore to see what we can discover. As we learn, we grow; and when we learn together, we also deepen our relationship by creating shared interests and fun memories.

My kids love going to the bookstore. Reading on the computer is great, but having your own book that you can touch and hold is something special. We go to the bookstore on birthdays and half-birthdays, during the Christmas season, before vacations, and for any other excuse we can generate. One of the reasons my kids enjoy bookstores is that they know I will almost always get them a book when we are there. I believe that buying books is investing in their education. I might say no to a lot of things, but I try to say yes to books as often as possible.

I want to take every opportunity to encourage my children to read.

Some kids are natural readers, but a lot of kids need an extra push. Here are some ideas to get you started:

① Provide a good example by reading regularly.

② Read to your children daily, beginning at birth.

③ Choose early reading material carefully, making sure it is colorful, fun, and age appropriate.

④ Start a family library by setting aside shelves or areas just for books; give each child a small bookcase to start his or her own personal library.

⑤ Listen to audio books as a family.

⑥ Look through the daily newspaper or a weekly news magazine and discuss interesting, intriguing, or noteworthy articles.

⑦ Set aside special places and times to read.

⑧ Subscribe to magazines that keep children's attention and feed their interests.

⑨ Respect your children's choice of reading material, but introduce books that may stretch their interests.

⑩ Take your children to libraries and bookstores often.

⑪ Involve your children in summer reading programs, book fairs, or community book clubs.

⑫ Get excited about books you are reading and talk about them.

⑬ Ask your kids to tell you about what they are reading.

⑭ Create family reading contests.

⑮ Take books or magazines with you on vacations, car trips, or wherever you think you might have free time.

⑯ Give your children books for birthdays and special occasions.

⑰ Place interesting books throughout your house.

⑱ Research authors of books your children are reading and share what you discover.

As you apply these ideas, remember that you need to keep reading fun. Don't make it a chore or an assignment; make it a passion. Don't push your children, but entice them to read. Those children who discover the joys of reading carry it with them throughout the rest of their lives.

TURN OFF THE TV

Television is the greatest invention of the human race.

At least that's what I thought when I was eight years old. If my parents had allowed it, I would have watched it every day from the moment I got home from school until I went to bed. One of the problems with television, however, is that it can become all-consuming and isolate family members from each other. It is easy to get so focused on our favorite shows that television begins to take priority over relationships. Communication is relegated to the commercials, and connection can't happen until the program is over.

Watching television has some built-in dangers. Because of this, the American Academy of Pediatrics recommends that children younger than two years old should not watch television and older children should not have television sets in their bedrooms. The AAP concludes that television viewing can affect the mental, social, and physical health of young people. Some of these dangers are:

- increased passivity

- increased obesity

- increased anxiety

- increased aggressiveness

- decreased creativity

- decreased social interaction

It's important to monitor these dangers in your children. For too long in our society, these issues have been left unaddressed. Your children are too precious for you to ignore the potential negative impacts of television. These dangers are most pronounced when your kids are watching too much TV and when what they are watching is inappropriate. Many popular programs today promote graphic violence, profanity, negative attitudes, unhealthy behavior, meanness, disrespect, and moral compromise. Somehow our culture has forgotten that children follow the example of what they observe. They mimic what they see on television, just as they mimic what they see in real life. So be aware of how much television your children watch and what shows they see.

Yet before you throw your television out, you need to know that it can be a positive tool in any family. It can provide entertainment, education, relaxation, and great family time. There are a lot of positive options on television, and your family can enjoy watching it together, especially if you set up some guidelines:

① Decide ahead of time what you want to watch, and turn off the TV when your show is over.

② Limit how much TV you and your children will watch each day.

③ Evaluate what you watch in terms of violence, language, sexual content, morality, faith, and general appropriateness.

④ Turn off the TV during meals.

⑤ Discourage solo watching.

⑥ Always make sure homework and chores are done before watching television.

⑦ Watch TV together as a family, making the time fun and interactive.

⑧ Talk about what you just watched, discussing its application to everyday life.

These suggestions help to minimize the dangers and maximize the positive aspects of television for your family. Many of them are also applicable for DVDs, computer games, and video game systems.

THE KEY IS TOGETHERNESS

Books bring families together. Whether you read to your children, talk about what they've read, or both read a book at the same time, make it a shared experience. People like to talk about what they've read. On the other hand, television tends to pull people inside themselves. It can be shared, but you usually have to be intentional about it. I have had wonderful times with my kids watching special programs or movies on television. The issue isn't that books are good and television is bad. We simply have to make healthy choices and keep a positive balance. Wherever you choose to focus your attention as a family, whether on books or TV, do it in a way that brings you closer together rather than pulling you apart.

TODAY'S TOOLS

Prayer

Dear God,

Thank you for the amazing power of words. Thank you for how they can teach, give understanding, direct, remind, develop character, strengthen, delight, impart wisdom, encourage, and comfort.

Help me to choose positive reading material for both my family and myself—material that will make us improved as individuals and healthier as a family and will draw us closer to you.

Help me to be a lifelong learner, with a continual desire to grasp and appreciate your miraculous universe and all it contains.

Inspire me to read your Word daily. Bring books into my life that will make me a better person, a better spouse, and a better parent.

Amen.

Passage

Listen to advice and accept instruction, and in the end you will be wise.
Proverbs 19:20

Practice

① Make a list of ten books you would like your children to read or you would like to read to them.

② Set up a family reading time that will happen at least once a week.

③ Visit a library or bookstore as a family sometime in the next week or two.

④ Find a television show that you can watch regularly together as a family. Also sit down with your spouse or somebody you respect to establish some healthy guidelines for watching television.

RULE ⓮
ESCAPE TOGETHER

I WAS SO EXCITED, I could hardly wait.

My parents had planned a road trip to Disneyland. They bought a travel trailer and packed it full of food, and we were off on our dream vacation. I must have been about ten at the time, with two younger sisters and a younger brother. None of us had ever been to Disneyland, but we heard that it was the happiest place on earth.

The drive from Portland, Oregon, to Anaheim, California, was going to be a three-day trip, but on the afternoon of the first day we ran into trouble. As we drove over the pass on the Oregon-California border, smoke began to pour out from under the hood of our car. Dad stopped and let the engine cool down. Then off we went again, but the smoke returned. We stopped and let the engine cool again, but this time the car wouldn't restart. Soon a tow truck pulled us into a small town, where a mechanic examined our car.

"The good news is that the engine is still under warranty," he said matter-of-factly. "The bad news is that it will take about a week for a new engine to get here."

My heart sank. *There goes our dream vacation.* Dad must have seen the disappointment in our eyes. He said, "Don't worry, we'll figure something out." Then he sent the four of us kids down the street to a movie theater. When the movie was over, Mom and Dad were waiting for us.

"We've got to hurry," Mom said.

"Why?" I asked.

"We're going to Disneyland," she said with a big smile.

We all cheered, and an hour later we boarded a Greyhound bus. Fourteen hours later we were in Anaheim, California. Disneyland was wonderful, and it was a fantastic vacation. We laughed and played and grew closer as a family, but that's not what I remember most. What I still carry with me today is that my parents made it happen. I knew that money was tight and six bus tickets weren't in the budget. But they were determined to make sure our family had a special getaway. They knew that vacations build great memories, and they didn't want us to miss the opportunity to share in this adventure.

Getaways are important for every family. They provide a wonderful environment for communication, and that is almost always positive. Even when vacations aren't positive, they are always memorable. Years later you will sit around with your children and laugh about the camping trip that was rained out or the road trip when the car broke down. Time softens the frustrations and leaves the golden treasures of shared experiences.

Once when the children were young, Tami and I went out to a restaurant and talked about family vacations. We made a list of places we would like to take the kids:

- Disneyland or Disney World

- the Grand Canyon

- Yellowstone

- Washington DC

- Mexico

- San Francisco

- Canada

Over the past ten years we have visited all but one of the places on our list. The last destination is Canada, and next August we are planning to spend a week in Victoria. My kids will tell you that these have been fantastic vacations. In fact, last week Dusty asked me, "When we grow up and get married, can we still come on family vacations?" I smiled and said, "Any time you want to join us on a family vacation, you can come." He smiled and said, "Thanks, Dad."

Family getaways used to feel like a waste of time and money, but now I realize they are one of my favorite things. Connections and experiences happen on vacations that can't happen anywhere else. Getaways are an investment in your children, your marriage, and your family—time you will never regret. There are three stages to these escapes.

PLANNING

A good plan begins with a good dream. It's fun to let your imagination run wild, considering all the fascinating and beautiful and exciting places you'd love to visit. Get your family together and ask everybody to share their dreams with each other. Encourage each person to make a list of three places he or she would like to go in the next year. Some might be easy to plan, such as a day at the zoo or a camping trip or a walk along the river. These are fun, inexpensive, and simple getaways. But then there are the big getaways.

These don't just happen. Big getaways take time, money, and long-term planning. But they are very much worth it. Tami and I make sure that money is set aside for a family getaway at least once a year. We are so committed to these escapes that we will stop going out to dinner, buying clothing, and making other purchases so we can save money for our big getaways. Our saying is, "Where there is a will, there has got to be a way." We even have a five-gallon coin jar where we toss all our loose change. It's amazing how much we can collect in a year. Yet big vacations can cost big money, so sometimes you have to scale down. One year our Disneyland getaway had to be postponed because the money just wasn't there. But we insisted on a getaway, so we took our tent trailer to the beach for a long weekend and still had a great time.

Once you have saved your money and chosen a destination for your big getaway, the fun really starts. Spend time together gathering brochures, reading maps, looking through travel books, and checking out Web sites. Talking and dreaming about your escape will make it seem so much more special, before you have even left the house.

Right now Dylan, Dusty, and I are planning a guy's escape to Washington DC. We can't wait for our adventure, even though Tami is wondering if it is safe to let her three boys loose in the world without her supervision. Dylan wants to go the Smithsonian and Six Flags amusement park. Dusty wants to see the FBI Headquarters and the Spy Museum. I just want to have a great time with my sons. We will leave in about a month, and every day we talk about our getaway. The anticipation is building, and Dylan sums it up with, "I can't wait!"

EXPERIENCING

Getaways come in many different flavors. Each person is unique, with different needs, expectations, and perspectives. Some families enjoy camping trips filled with hiking, boating, fishing, and sitting around a campfire. Other families like to take road trips that lead to a different place each night. Then there are the relaxing getaways, in which families sleep in, read good books, and do little or nothing. I also know families who think educational getaways are the very best. Wherever they go, they love to learn about history, geography, or wildlife. One more type of escape is the adventurous getaway, exploring anything from the Mayan ruins of Mexico to Disney World to your nearest big city to whatever point of interest lies within a ten-mile radius of your home.

Every family needs to periodically escape from schedules, responsibilities, telephones, and all the other things that make life so hectic. When you are away from it all, it is easier to truly connect with one another. To make this connection the best it can possibly be, try to include these six ideas somewhere in every getaway:

- Love. Spend time showing each other how much you appreciate your family.

- Relax. Let go of your worries and stressors, put up your feet, and take it easy.

- Laugh. Don't take everything so seriously; play and have fun; see if you can get others to laugh till their sides hurt.

- Flex. Even if things don't go as you wished or expected, you can still have a fun time.

- Learn. Do your best to discover something you didn't know about your surroundings and each member of your family.

- Stretch. Be willing to try new things and experiences.

Above all, be positive and connect, for these special moments are treasures your family will never forget.

REMEMBERING

Planning and experiencing getaways are great, but remembering them is my favorite time. I love to reminisce about riding on the California Screamin' roller coaster at Disneyland, enjoying the sun as it filtered through the ancient trees of the redwood forest, and taking surf lessons in the sparkling blue ocean in Mexico. I have thousands of these memories, and each time I recall them I recapture a magic moment that my family shared together.

Memories are a powerful link between family members, and getaways are a great way to make sure these memories are positive. As we race through the frustrations and franticness of everyday life, little reminders can take us back to those wonderful memories. Whenever Tami and I see a horse, she leans toward me and whispers, "His name is Rambo." Suddenly our minds are transported back to a great vacation in Puerto Vallarta.

Tami enjoys horseback riding, while I know very little about it. At a ranch outside Puerto Vallarta, Tami rode Strawberry and I rode Rambo. The names of these two horses perfectly fit their personalities. Strawberry was gentle and slow and compliant. Rambo was wild and fast and independent. Rambo galloped everywhere at full speed, and I learned quickly to hold on to the horn of the saddle with both hands and pray that I wouldn't die. Apparently I wasn't the most graceful-looking cowboy on the ranch, for when I looked over at Tami she was laughing so hard she almost fell off her horse. Now she periodically reminds me of Rambo and my remarkable equestrian style.

I'm sure you have your special memories of getaways too. Treasure these times. Talk about them often to friends and to each other. Don't ever forget them. During my family's getaways, I have learned to appreciate each person even more than in our everyday lives. These getaways strengthen our family and leave us with wonderful memories that we will reminisce about the rest of our lives.

Getaways are to a family what shocks are to a car. You can travel without them, but you will feel every bump. When you have shocks, your journey is smoother and quieter and much more enjoyable.

TODAY'S TOOLS

Prayer

Dear God,

When life gets hectic and crazy and overwhelming, lead me away with my family to a place of fun and laughter and relaxation. Let me rest in green meadows beside peaceful streams.

Encourage me to get away with my children, to escape together, to create an adventure.

Help me to play more often.

Help me to plan more vacations.

Help me to look for more opportunities.

Help me to enjoy more experiences. Help me to build more memories.

Forgive me for letting the worries and weight and work of life keep me from focusing on my family. Don't let me ever forget the value of my children and the joy of getting away with them.

Amen.

Passage

Our mouths were filled with laughter, our tongues with songs of joy.
Psalm 126:2

Practice

① Sit down with your spouse or a good friend and list eight escapes you would like to take with your kids before they reach the age of twenty.

② Call a family meeting to plan all the details of a vacation to take place sometime in the next eighteen months.

③ Consider how the six getaway words applied to your last escape:

> *love*
>
> *relax*
>
> *laugh*

flex

learn

stretch

④ Gather pictures, maps, and mementos from past escapes and make a getaway scrapbook.

RULE ⑮
COOL DOWN

"I CAN'T CONTROL MY TEMPER," Lydia said.

"What does your anger look like?" I asked.

"I yell and scream and sometimes throw things. I feel like a volcano that blows up and hurts everybody around me. I hate it, but when I explode it's like I don't even care. I'm just mad and you'd better get out of my way."

"How long have you been angry?"

"I rarely lost my temper until I had kids. Then I turned into my father. I hated it when he got angry, and I swore that I'd never do what he did. But here I am twenty years later, just like Dad." She covered her face with her hands and started to cry. "I've been scared of my dad's anger my whole life, and now I'm doing the same thing to my kids."

"Lydia, you've just taken the first step," I said. "You've admitted your anger, and you want to find a better way to express it. That is a fantastic start."

Everybody gets angry. Some have a short fuse; others have an incredibly patient disposition and seldom get upset. Anger has a lot of faces. It can be cold or fiery, totally silent or deafening. It can be frightening or ridiculous, pouty or pushy. It can also be hurtful or understandable.

Anger is a confusing emotion for most adults—and even more confusing for your children.

We all have our own things that make us mad—bad drivers, selfish people, high prices, stupid mistakes, broken promises. Yet of all the situations that trigger people's frustrations and tempers, family is toward the top of the list. Every family produces those special irritations that can spark a fire as quickly as a match in a dry forest. Often it is easier for parents to be more patient and tolerant of other children than of their own kids. Some of the most common family triggers are:

- disobedience

- hitting and fighting

- yelling and screaming

- disrespect

- stealing

- lying

- foul language

- cruelty

- poor grades

- defiance

- laziness

- stubbornness

I'm sure you can think of a lot more, because kids seem to be creative in their ability to do things that irritate.

Though anger is a normal emotion, it rarely gets a parent what he or she wants. In fact, anger usually makes a situation worse. The apostle Paul wrote, "In your anger do not sin" (Ephesians 4:26). Anger controls you when it becomes too intense, lasts too long, or makes your thinking too cloudy. Over and over I see kids and teenagers in my office who are in trouble with their parents. Usually I ask something such as, "Why have you gotten grounded for the next two years?" The answer is often, "Because Mom got really angry" or "Dad gets mad a lot."

"But why did they get so upset?" I ask.

"I don't know," is the most common response.

After having this conversation several hundred times, I came to the conclusion that most kids can only process one communication level at a time. They can either focus on your words or your emotions, not both at the same time. Ninety percent of the time they hear your emotions, while your words go right over their heads. Therefore if you want your child to get your message, you need to swallow hard and deal with your anger. Try the following principles:

① Admit your anger. If you're angry, be honest with yourself about it. Don't ignore it, deny it, or stuff it. Face this emotion and choose to control it, rather than letting it control you.

② Evaluate your anger. Ask yourself, "What just happened? Why am I so upset? What is the source of this anger? What is the healthy thing to do right now?"

③ Choose your perception. Catch your breath and put the problem in perspective. Look at the situation in as positive a light as you can. Don't minimize the problem, but don't make it bigger than it really is.

④ Calm yourself. If your anger is getting out of control, lower your voice, sit down, and breathe deeply. If you still can't calm down, remove yourself from the situation.

⑤ Watch your words. When you're angry, it is easy to say things you will later regret. Watch what you say; once those words are out of your mouth, you can never take them back.

⑥ Work out your anger. Anger produces adrenaline, and adrenaline seeks release. You need to exert energy in order to work out your anger. Go for a drive, weed a garden, chop wood, write a letter, or take a walk.

⑦ Talk about your anger. Describe how you feel to a safe person. Be direct and honest without blaming or attacking. If you're overreacting, admit it. The better you can communicate about your anger, the more you can control it.

⑧ Resolve your anger. Commit yourself to not letting the sun go down on your anger. The longer you hold on to it, the worse it gets. Unresolved anger turns into bitterness, meanness, or depression. So learn to let go and move on.

⑨ Seek help. If your anger persists or is out of control, get help. You don't want your anger to push your family away. Talk to a counselor, pastor, or physician in order to develop an anger management plan.

If you can deal with your anger, you can probably deal with just about anything.

Let's get back to Lydia.

During the time that I counseled her, we talked about all nine of the above points, but we spent most of our time talking about how she could calm herself down. She needed practical, hands-on ideas to de-escalate her emotions. The strategy that seemed to work best for Lydia was to sit down on the floor right in front of the child she was angry with. When she sat face-to-face at the same level as her child, she found it harder to rant and rave. When she was standing and pacing and swinging around her arms, it was easy for her anger to escalate, and in turn, scare her kids.

As Lydia sat in front of her child, she pulled herself together. She did this by:

- breathing deeply

- praying

- speaking gently

- looking into her child's eyes

- listening

- talking to herself

Lydia told me that talking to herself was the most important step in the process. She used to say things to herself such as: *How could she do this to me? Why would he do such a mean, insensitive, rude thing?* Yet this sort of negative self-talk just got her more upset. So she started quoting verses to herself: *Be quick to listen, slow to speak and slow to become angry* (James 1:19); *A fool gives full vent to his anger* (Proverbs 29:11); *Stirring up anger produces strife* (Proverbs

30:33). This positive self-talk seemed to make all the difference in the world, at least until the car crisis.

On a beautiful fall day, Lydia's seven-year-old son accidentally ran his bicycle into the side of her new car. The result was a three-foot scratch that cut right to the metal. Lydia loved her new car. She knew this was an accident, but she also knew it could have been easily avoided if he'd been more careful. She was furious, but she bit her tongue. Lydia knew if she said anything, it probably would not be the right thing. So this time she gave herself a time-out. She removed herself totally from the situation so she could regain her composure. She went to her bedroom, shut the door, and focused on calming down by praying.

This time her self-talk had to be more direct and personal. She cut right to the core of the issue by saying things such as, "My son is more important than my car," "It is just a car," and "I can get my car repaired." At first her words held little conviction, but the more she repeated them, the more she believed them. Within fifteen minutes she regained control and could deal with her son.

Every parent has moments when he or she needs to step back from a situation. Distance can help you regain your objectivity and handle a frustration without regret. When you take a self-imposed time-out, consider one or more of the following ways of redirecting your anger:

- listening to relaxing music

- reading a book

- taking a bath or shower

- praying

- calling a friend

- writing in a journal

- talking to yourself

Anger can cause you to lash out physically and verbally in ways that leave permanent scars. Last week I spoke to a young lady who had not seen her mother in ten years, though they both live in the same town. When I asked her what had caused such a rift, she said, "I hate her. She was always angry. I could deal with how she called me names and pulled my hair, but when she did it to my little brother, that was it. My mother is unsafe, and I can't deal with her temper. It just hurts too much."

Too many parent-child relationships are damaged because of anger. Words are said that can't be unsaid. When you are upset, everybody is miserable. Your anger is rarely worth the damage it can do.

PUTTING OUT FIRES

"What in the world are you doing?"

"I don't know," said Chris's son.

"Why is your room such a disaster?" Chris yelled as he grabbed his son by the arm.

"I'll clean it tomorrow."

"No," Chris said, "you'll clean it right now."

"But I'm tired," the boy said as he tried to wiggle out of his father's grip.

"I don't care how tired you are!" Chris gripped tighter. "I told you to do something, and if you don't do it, you'll be sorry."

"Why are you so mean to me?" The boy started crying. "All you do is yell and scream at me. Nothing I do is ever right."

Unfortunately, the situation got a lot worse as emotions escalated and harsh words turned cruel. As I spoke to Chris the next day, he told me how irrational he had become, even though he loved his son very much.

"What went wrong?" I asked.

"I had just gotten home," said Chris. "It was eleven o'clock at night and I was exhausted. Work had been crazy, and I took out my frustration on my son. Sure, his room was a mess, but that wasn't the real problem."

"What was the real problem?"

"I was," Chris said, as the tears streamed down his face.

Family life can be a challenge. Maybe that's why James Dobson insists that "parenting isn't for cowards." As parents we need to be strong, steady, and sensitive. We need to control our tempers and make sure we do our best to make difficult situations better. No, we aren't perfect. There are times we pour gasoline on a hot spot and act surprised when it bursts into flames. Anger can easily spread a fire. But as role models for our children, we need to learn how to manage our anger. As we do this, we will find that we are putting out fires rather than spreading them.

TODAY'S TOOLS

Prayer

Dear God,

Sometimes my kids can get me so frustrated that I say or do or think things that are not the best. Forgive me when I am short tempered or hot-headed.

Show me how to manage my anger by not overreacting, by watching my words, and by believing the best.

Remind me that anger rarely gets me what I want and frequently makes a situation worse.

Keep me from rage, hostility, sarcasm, revenge, bitterness, and grudge keeping.

Keep me calm and slow to anger. Give me a peace and patience when things do not go as they should. As situations around me heat up, touch my heart and help me cool down.

Amen.

Passage

A quick-tempered man does foolish things. . . . Wise men turn away anger. Proverbs 14:17; 29:8

Practice

① Consider the situations in your family that are most likely to trigger your temper.

② Talk to a friend about the nine principles of anger listed in this chapter, and determine which of the points you struggle with most.

③ Sit down with your family and explore what is best at calming you down.

RULE 16
MANAGE YOUR STRESS

I LOVE MY KIDS.

But sometimes they drive me crazy. They yell. They cry. They fight. They break things. They make messes. They do a hundred things that don't make any sense. Then when I ask them, "Why?" they give me an answer such as, "I didn't do it" or "I don't know." By this time I'm ready to send them to Antarctica for the winter, but then they do something wonderful and I melt.

The most frustrating thing about children is that they act childish. A child is not a little adult. Even if they have delightful moments of maturity, they are still kids. How is it that a child can totally tear apart a room in five minutes, but it takes him two hours to clean it up? There are certain things about children that just *are*. Most children are loud, get wild, hit each other, throw tantrums, need constant reminders, and act before they think. These sorts of things drive most parents crazy.

Though we honestly love our kids, they can easily bring out the worst in us. Our children stress us out and wear us out. Yet when they see us reacting this way, they feel insecure, and their negative behavior tends to escalate. Then we are really in trouble. To have a great family, we must be able to manage these issues. It's hard to connect in a positive way when you are stressed or exhausted.

DE-STRESS

We live in a world where we go as fast as we can and pack in as much as we can. Most of us experience stress every day, especially when we feel overwhelmed. For many parents, loud noises and uncontrolled activity trigger an increase in their stress level. These sound like characteristics of most kids!

Some parents have become so accustomed to high levels of stress that they no longer recognize how stressed they are, but the rest of their family does. Stress makes a person impatient, negative, and easily upset. Other common symptoms of someone who is stressed are:

- forgetfulness or absentmindedness

- frequent headaches or stomach pains

- distraction or lack of focus

- being overly emotional

- short temper

- lack of motivation

- unhappiness

- desire to escape

If you are experiencing more than two or three of these symptoms, it's time to reduce your stress.

"I know how to reduce my stress," said Sarah, a mother of three children under the age of five.

"How?" I asked.

"Go on a monthlong vacation without my kids."

Sarah would do anything for her kids, but we all have our breaking points. Many mothers feel the highest levels of stress when they have children under five. Fathers often feel the stress more when their kids are in their teenage years. Both of these are tough stages in a family, but you will survive. Yet if you learn to reduce your stress level, you will feel better about yourself, and your kids will feel better about you as well. Here are a few ideas to help you:

> *Slow down.* You don't have to race. Everything doesn't have to be done today. The reality is that the faster you go, the more tired and impatient you get. Stop and enjoy the moment. Take a break and take a deep breath. Going faster rarely makes you a better parent. In fact, as it stresses you out, it stresses everybody else in your family as well.

> *Simplify.* Life is full of clutter and complications. We pack our lives with too much, and then we desperately try to figure out how to squeeze in just one more thing. The key is to eliminate. Simplify your schedule by saying no more often. If you don't have time, don't do it. Then simplify your space by getting rid of stuff you don't need or don't use.

> *Focus.* Figure out what is really important to you and make that your priority. Keeping a clean house, finishing projects, washing dishes, and doing laundry are all important things, but spending quality time with your family is even more

important. Your child is more valuable than any of the other distractions that so easily consume your time.

Enjoy. Do things that refresh your spirit and lighten your heart. Take the time to relax with a positive escape—watch a sunset, read a book, fill a hot bath, play a game. You might also find a hobby that reduces your stress: painting, gardening, walking, golfing, or whatever. Enjoyment washes the stress from your body and mind, reenergizing you for all that follows.

Seek. When you are overwhelmed, go to God. He can calm the roughest storm. There are times that every parent needs God's strength, peace, or wisdom. Going to God in prayer, whether for a quick moment or a longer period of time, can refresh and renew you like nothing else. Meditating on Scriptures that soothe the soul can change your perspective and set you back on course.

Connect. Reach out and spend time with other parents. Share your thoughts and ask their opinions. Talk out your tensions with a trusted friend. Sometimes we all need a support system to get perspective, encouragement, and help. When we are able to vent and problem solve with friends, we are reminded that we are not alone. Besides, sharing a burden with others makes it feel so much lighter.

By reducing your stress, you become a healthier person, a more positive spouse, and a better parent. When you take care of yourself, you are really taking care of your kids.

Stress ultimately leads to exhaustion. There is only so much you can do before the stress starts to affect you negatively. Stress is like a clog in the gas line of your car—it makes you cough and sputter and leaves you without the power you need to move forward. It's time to admit that you can't do it all. There is a breaking point when all the stress you have accumulated over the past month tumbles down, burying you under a crushing burden of exhaustion. On days like this you don't even want to crawl out of bed. When you do get up, everything feels like it takes too much effort. You just want to find a comfortable chair and let the world pass you by, but all the responsibilities and chores of parenthood won't let you get away with this. So you force yourself to your feet and try your best to do your everyday activities. Yet it often feels like you are just going through the motions—your head is fuzzy and your body is numb. The solution to this may be surprisingly simple.

GET A GOOD NIGHT'S SLEEP

Most people need at least eight hours of restful sleep each night, yet for many parents this doesn't happen. You stay up late trying to get everything done, then when you crawl into bed, exhausted and eager for sleep, your brain won't shut off. It is racing a hundred miles an hour— solving problems, making lists, reviewing frustrations, preparing for the next day, and worrying about any number of concerns.

Finally, when you do get to sleep, you risk a restless night, an early wake-up without being able to get back to sleep, or awaking just as exhausted as when you laid your head on your pillow.

You need your sleep. Exhaustion leads to stress, which increases your potential anger, which makes it harder to sleep. Thus the cycle continues in a downward spiral. Sleep is crucial to our general well-being and our ability to be good parents. Sleep helps you:

- refresh your spirit

- reenergize your body

- readjust your attitude

- recapture your sanity

- reduce your frustrations

- rejuvenate your happiness

- relax your tensions

- restore your health

- remember your positives

- regain your emotional stability

- resolve your challenges

- renew your confidence

Sleep is such a simple solution, but because there is so much to do, parents frequently try to get by on less rest than they need.

You can energize yourself best by being intentional and protective about your sleep. Fight for it, because when you're worn out life loses its luster, and the everyday challenges of your family can become a crisis. Here are a few strategies that the sleep experts use:

① Schedule enough sleep. If you need eight hours of sleep, schedule eight hours. A good rule of thumb is that if you have to use an alarm clock to wake up, you aren't getting enough sleep.

② Establish a pattern. Go to bed at the same time each night. Your body needs to get used to shutting down at a predetermined time.

③ Turn off the television. Too many parents close their day by watching the news, which is frequently stressful and depressing. Television is rarely calming. So turn it off and turn on some relaxing music instead.

④ Get comfortable. Make sure your bed—mattress, sheets, and pillows—allows you to relax. We spend almost a third of our lives in bed, so invest appropriately. Also make sure that what you wear to sleep in is comfortable.

⑤ Create an atmosphere. Make your bedroom relaxing. De-clutter it—clutter creates tension. Dim it—light keeps you awake. Discover it—find what it takes to make your room comfortable in terms of appearance, smell, temperature, and noise.

⑥ Prepare yourself. Most people can't go from wide awake to sleep without a winding-down period. So set aside at least thirty minutes to take a bath, read a book, pray—anything that will ease you into rest.

⑦ Avoid stimulation. Avoid caffeine or exercise during the six hours before bed. And avoid heavy foods, intense arguments, and loud noises during the two hours before bed.

It's important to be intentional about getting a good night's sleep, because the bottom line is simple: Every great family needs its rest.

HOLD ON TO HOPE

Sleep energizes you and dispels your exhaustion. It also helps you handle more stress without breaking down. If you are tired or sleep deprived, even minor stressors can push you over the edge. But when you are well rested, you can handle all those little frustrations with more patience and grace than usual.

When we are stressed or worn out, we tend to overreact or underreact to our children. Stress and exhaustion warp our perspective, making us less effective as parents. Everybody gets stressed or worn out at times. What is important is that you notice it and do something about it.

Suzy was an exuberant twenty-six-year-old who had always dreamed of being a mother. She had two of the most adorable little girls I had ever seen, but they had more energy than Suzy. By the time she took care of them all day and completed the many chores of a stay-at-home mom, she was spent. Some days, it seemed as if it was all she could do to just hold on until her husband came home at five o'clock. Over time she lost her bubbly smile and sunny disposition. She became the sort of negative, uninvolved parent she didn't respect. She was so stressed she couldn't relax, discipline the kids, or even have fun. Suzy was completely worn out, but she didn't have the energy to do anything about it.

Suzy was not happy. So she decided it was time to do something to manage her stress—for herself, her husband, and her kids. She started by simply saying no to all new commitments for a month and going to bed a half hour earlier than normal. This felt so good that the next month she tried two more de-stressing activities.

"At least it's a start," Suzy said. "There are a lot more things I can try, but you've got to begin somewhere."

Suzy still looks stressed, but at least now she smiles. I've met thousands of Suzys—great parents who are so stressed and frazzled that they feel miserable. You might even be one of them. Don't give up. There is hope. As you learn to de-stress and get some quality sleep, you will be surprised at how life looks brighter and your parenting improves. Suddenly you feel better and your family is a lot happier.

TODAY'S TOOLS

Prayer

Dear God,

Kids create stress. Chores create stress. Responsibilities create stress. Life creates stress. Yet you tell us to be anxious for nothing. When life is overwhelming . . .

Teach me to slow down.

Show me how to simplify.

Help me to focus on what is truly important.

Lead me to times of relaxation and refreshment.

Remind me to go to you.

Encourage me to reach out and connect with others.

When I am tired and stressed, keep me from taking it out on my family through impatience or negativity.

Create in me a calm heart, a renewed spirit, and a rested body.

Thank you for being the Prince of Peace and promising to give us a peace that passes all understanding.

Amen.

Passage

Cast all your anxiety on him because he cares for you.
1 Peter 5:7

Practice

1. Consider how stress affects you and what symptoms you experience when the pressure is high.
2. List your greatest stressors during the past week. Write beside each stressor one thing you might do to help you relax.
3. Evaluate your recent sleep patterns by asking yourself the following questions:

   How well did I sleep last night?

   How many hours of sleep do I tend to get?

   What makes it hard for me to get a good night's sleep?

   What helps me sleep the best?

RULE ⑰
FIGHT KINDLY

I COULDN'T WAIT TO GET HOME.

I'd been gone for the weekend, and I missed my family. I wanted to kiss Tami and hug my kids. I wanted all of us to be together—laughing, playing, connecting. But life rarely goes as smoothly as I think it should.

What happened?

Little brothers like to bug big brothers and big brothers blow up and everything escalates. Within an hour of my return home, Dusty was crying in his room and wouldn't come out. Dylan felt like nobody understood him and that we all let Dusty get away with whatever he wanted. Tami was mad at me for not handling it the way she thought I should have, and I was left sitting alone on the couch thinking, *All I wanted was a nice, happy, fun evening with my family.*

Why can't everybody just get along?

Maybe I'm an idealist, but I want a world where everything is calm and nobody disagrees. I hate fights. Yet in reality, every family fights. They fight about toys or television or money. They fight about who said what or what happened when. The apostle James asked the church why they were fighting. Then he answered his own question with this reason: "You want something but don't get it" (James 4:2). To put it simply, we fight because we want things to always go our way.

Most fights are silly. We don't tend to fight about high moral principles; we fight about little things that are usually selfish, stupid, or irrelevant. Yet in the middle of the conflict, our position seems so important. We grow stubborn and dig in. Some families fight with loud words; others fight with silence. Some families fight often; others save up their frustration for a big explosion. Some families are direct and confrontational; others hint and pick and complain. Yet healthy families know how to fight kindly. They might argue and disagree, but they do it with respect, remembering these ten things not to do:

- no hitting
- no name calling
- no yelling
- no insulting
- no threatening
- no humiliating
- no pushing
- no blaming
- no refusing to talk
- no swearing

We all know that we shouldn't do these things, but as emotions heat up, so does the fight.

FIGHTS BETWEEN PARENTS

Whenever you put two people together, sooner or later they will find something to fight about. If those two people are married with children, the probability of conflict increases significantly. Common fights involve:

Sex: There isn't a good time without interruption or you're too tired.

Money: There isn't enough or you have different priorities on spending it, saving it, or investing it.

Family: Extended family members get too involved or you just see things differently than they do.

Chores: You disagree about who does what around the house, how they do it, and how often.

Communications: There isn't a good time to talk or you don't like your partner's communication style.

Anger: There is a disagreement on the appropriate expression of anger toward you or the children.

Lifestyle: There is some lifestyle difference with which you feel uncomfortable or frustrated.

Preferences: Your likes and dislikes are not the same as your spouse's.

Relationship: One or both of you are not happy with the direction the marriage is going.

Parenting: You have different styles of and approaches to raising your children.

These are good things to fight about, as long as you get somewhere. Unfortunately, too many couples go around and around on the same old issues, without getting anywhere. They get no closer to resolution or conclusion; they simply get more frustrated and desperate. This need not be so.

The goal of a kind fight is to understand each other better and discover some point of compromise or resolution. Fights don't have to be negative. They are only bad if they do more damage than good. Remember, your kids are watching and listening. Even though they are in the backseat, the door is closed, or you are speaking softly, they are still keenly aware of what's going on. Kids are smart and they know more about your conflicts than you might think.

A healthy fight between parents can be good for your kids to observe. It shows them that conflict doesn't have to be a crisis and it doesn't have to end badly. It also teaches them how to fight kindly. A fair fight conducted with respect and honesty can be a positive example. So when you fight, pretend that every word and tone of your voice is being recorded. Watch what you say. Show your children how to fight and compromise and find resolution and make up. Let them know that a good fight can have a happy ending.

FIGHTS BETWEEN SIBLINGS

Children with no brothers or sisters have unique advantages and disadvantages. One of their greatest disadvantages is that they have no sibling with whom to argue and fight. This has the potential of leaving them unprepared to deal with the everyday conflicts that occur on the job, among neighbors, in friendships, or throughout marriage. Sibling conflict is an aspect of family life that is especially frustrating for parents. If your kids are like most, they have moments when they act like best friends. Then they have moments of hostility, when you are forced to intervene: "Keep your hands to yourself," "Are you trying to start a fight?" "Just be nice," or "Why did you say that?"

When siblings disagree, it provides a wonderful educational opportunity. Here are some of the things sibling rivalry teaches your children:

- It shows them that life doesn't always go their way.

- It encourages them to work with others using basic social skills.

- It forces them to develop healthy problem-solving strategies.

- It teaches them that there are consequences to all they say and do.

- It impresses upon them the importance of "fighting fair."

Now don't get me wrong—I'm not promoting sibling rivalry. I'm not even saying it's a good thing. I'm simply recognizing that it has a positive side.

Without direction and intervention, fighting between your children can become mean, hurtful, and abusive. It can escalate to a point at which it leaves scars. Conflict needs to be managed. Your kids need to know what is acceptable and what is not acceptable. Yet at the same time, you don't want to be constantly correcting and controlling them. Like so many things in life, there is a balance between too much distance and too much involvement. The following ten principles will point you in the right direction:

1. Expect conflict. Different children will have different opinions, needs, habits, personalities, and moods. To expect no conflict is unrealistic.

2. Create family rules. Regularly repeat certain rules about how to treat each other, what is unacceptable, and how to solve certain problems.

3. Anticipate tension times. Children have times when they are more prone to conflict, such as when they are tired, hungry, or overwhelmed.

4. Give a warning. When you see things escalating, calmly tell your kids that if rules are broken there will be consequences.

5. Avoid being a referee. Don't step into conflicts unless things get out of control. Encourage children to settle their own disagreements.

6. Stay calm. Don't jump to conclusions, react too quickly, or let your kids pull you down to their level.

7. Listen. Take the time to listen to each side of the conflict, letting each child know that you understand his or her perspective.

8. Share your expectations. Communicate clearly what you would like to see, reminding them of times in the past when they have handled things well.

⑨ Brainstorm solutions. Help your children come up with various ways to resolve the conflict so that everybody involved feels okay with the solution.

⑩ If stuck, separate. Sometimes children need some distance to let their frustrations subside and emotions cool down. Give them time apart and then try to resolve the issue.

These principles won't solve every problem. They might not even reduce the fighting, but they will increase the chance that your kids will learn something from their childhood conflicts.

Just because your kids fight, it doesn't mean that they don't love and appreciate each other. Yet sometimes as parents, we have to remind our children of this. Dusty loves to bug his big brother, and Dylan doesn't always handle this very well. The two of them can yell, hit, push, and break every one of the ten rules mentioned earlier about what not to do. Yet Dusty constantly wants to spend time with his big brother, and Dylan says that the scariest event in his life was when he thought Dusty might die because of a burst appendix.

The challenge for most parents is getting our kids to encourage one another rather than attack. Nicholas Sparks and his brother, Micah, address this in their memoir, *Three Weeks with My Brother*. When they were growing up, their mother grew tired of their fighting. So every night as she tucked the boys into bed, she asked them to tell her three things they liked about each other. They write that sometimes this was difficult, but that the simple exercise was responsible for the close relationship they now share, three decades later.

As a psychologist, I find that many people come to me because they are having a conflict with someone they love. What I have discovered over the years is that almost every fight can be solved kindly. We just have to remember that love is more important than winning.

TODAY'S TOOLS

Prayer

Dear God,

Whenever there are disagreements or conflicts in our family, help us all to fight kindly.

Forgive me for the times I get so wrapped up in winning that I forget about my spouse's feelings. Forgive me for my selfishness, insensitivity, and stubbornness.

Forgive me for the times I get so upset with my children's conflicts that I let them pull me down to their level. Forgive me for reacting to my children in such a way that I frighten them, frustrate them, or fuel their insecurities.

Remind me that you are more concerned with how I handle conflict than whether I am right. Empower me to show your love, peace, patience, and gentleness in the midst of our family differences.

Teach me how to resolve every fight graciously. Soften my heart and open my eyes to what would be best for the family, not just what I want.

Amen.

Passage

Do not repay anyone evil for evil. Be careful to do what is right in the eyes of everybody.
Romans 12:17

Practice

① Gather your family together to determine what sort of "fair fighting" rules would be best for your home. Discuss each of the ten things not to do listed in this chapter, and choose your top five to include in your family rules.

② Consider any unresolved conflict you might currently have with your spouse or children. Commit yourself to doing what you can to resolve these difficulties today in a way that will be healthy and healing.

③ Identify potential hot spots for conflict in your family. Then brainstorm how you can avoid these troubles and what to do if you get trapped in them.

RULE **⑱**
PRAY FOR THEM

PRAYER WORKS.

Kids know this. When they are scared, they want you to pray. When somebody is hurt, they want you to pray. When they are ready for bed, they want you to pray.

"Daddy, pray that nothing bad will happen."

"Mom, will you pray for Grandpa?"

"You've got to pray before I can go to sleep."

Dusty likes me to pray, but he doesn't want me to put him on the spot. One evening when our family was eating at a restaurant, I said, "Dusty, why don't you pray for the meal?"

He gave me a dirty look but bowed his head and started praying. "Dear Lord, please help my dad to not ask me to pray. Show him that I don't like it when he does this. It makes me mad at him. So bless our food. Amen."

As Dusty knows (but may not always admit), when you care about someone, you pray for that person. In a world of dangers, temptations, and challenges, your kids desperately need your prayers. This may be the most important thing you do all day—more important than paperwork, lunch meetings, golf, television, laundry, yard work. Your kids are gifts from God, and you need to treat them as such. I do not believe anyone can successfully parent without God's grace. Not only do your prayers protect your children in ways you will probably never know, they also strengthen the following bonds:

- Your bond with God. The more you talk to him, the closer you will feel to him.

- Your bond with your kids. Praying for them reminds you of their needs and emotionally pulls you closer.

- Your kids' bond with you. When they know you are praying for them, they feel protected and loved by you.

As you consider the power of these three bonds, you might ask what is keeping you from praying more. Prayer is a pleasure, especially when it involves praying for those we love. C. S. Lewis calls this "a sweet duty." Praying for my kids feels so good and so right, but it's easy for me to get distracted. So before I even start to pray for my kids, I pray for myself. I pray that I can be the best parent possible. To do this I often pray for the "ten p's." I pray that I have:

1. purpose: pointing my kids in the right direction
2. peace: staying calm when they frustrate me
3. perspective: seeing things from God's viewpoint
4. protectiveness: guarding them from what I can
5. positive words: encouraging them every chance I get
6. passion: being committed to God, my spouse, and them
7. patience: letting things happen in God's timing

⑧ provision: giving them their basic needs
⑨ purity: modeling the right words, actions, and attitudes
⑩ perseverance: showing love over the long haul

If I can get these ten qualities down, I can be a good parent. But I know myself too well. I know that every day I fail in all ten of these areas. I want to be a good parent, but I can't do it alone. So I have to lean on God and ask for his help. That's just the way it is.

Once I've prayed for myself, here are some of the things I try to pray about regarding my kids:

> *Their health.* It is so easy to take good health for granted, until something threatens it. Some children seem naturally healthy, while others struggle with minor illnesses, major diseases, or various handicaps. Pray that their bodies will be strong. When Dusty was ten years old, his appendix burst and he was hospitalized for ten days. Poisons spread and he lost too much weight. The only thing we could do for our son at that time was to pray.

> *Their safety.* The evening news makes me nervous with its coverage of car accidents, child molesters, kidnappings, drownings, shootings, and all sorts of horrible things. I wish I could always be there in every situation to keep my children safe. I can't, but God can. Pray for your child's protection and safety, because the world is full of danger. Yet know that God is the great protector.

Their choices. Life is full of choices—some good and some bad, some wise and some foolish. Pray that your children will make the right choices. Pray that immaturity, inexperience, peer pressure, and negative influences won't leave permanent scars. Pray that God will lead them to wise individuals who will help them make good choices. Pray that their choices will lead them to an abundant life that will please the Lord.

Their temptations. Every child has weaknesses that can easily open them up to unhealthy temptations. They might struggle with greed, people pleasing, alcohol, drugs, food, lying, cruelty, or laziness, to name a few. What is a temptation to one child might not be a problem for another. Pray for your children's specific struggles, and don't give up on them, even if they are not always successful in battling these temptations.

Their contentment. I want my kids to be a lot more than happy. Happiness is fleeting, based upon circumstances and comfort. Contentment comes from the heart and is not determined by how well your day went or how people respond to you. Contentment lives in a place of joy, peace, and fulfillment. It sees beyond the surface and allows you to weather difficulties without turning bitter. Pray that your children will learn contentment in all circumstances.

Their faith. A life without faith is empty and lonely and lost. Pray that your children will meet God early in life. Pray that they will learn to submit to God and actively resist Satan in all circumstances. Faith has an impact on every area of your child's life. Pray that your children will know how much God loves them and realize that they can do all things through Christ who strengthens them.

Their friends. As your children get older, their friends have an increasingly significant influence on their attitude, activities, and choices. Some friends are healthy and others are unhealthy. Pray that your children will be drawn to the right kind of friends and be protected from the wrong kind.

Their character. Someone once said that "good character is more valuable than gold." Character does the right thing. Character lives a life of compassion, integrity, kindness, generosity, goodness, humility, patience, courage, and self-control. Pray that your children will be caught when guilty and rewarded when good. Pray that they will learn early the value of doing the right thing.

Their future mate. Right now, your child's life partner is probably already out there somewhere. Pray for this person's health, safety, choices, temptations, contentment, faith, friends, and character, just as you have prayed for these things for your child. Also pray that your child will be kept from the wrong mate and saved for the right one. Too many people choose a spouse based on chemistry, physical appearance, or sexual attraction. Pray that your child will look deeper.

Their legacy. I hope my children will pass on to their children positive values, good character, and strong faith. Pray that your children will leave a legacy that God will reward not only in the lives of future generations but also in heaven. Pray that your children will think beyond the here and now. Pray that they will develop an eternal perspective and in so doing that they will leave a legacy that will please God and make this world a better place.

Your prayers will make a difference. They will accomplish amazing things. They might not make everything perfect, for God's ways are different from our ways. Your children might be resistant to your prayers and choose a different way, but don't stop praying. Prayer changes us, it changes our children, and it changes the world. Several years ago as our family was taking a road trip to southern Oregon, I asked my kids about prayer. All three told me that they liked to pray, but not too much. As we talked, we made up a game. We went through the alphabet and tried to say something about prayer with each letter. This is what we came up with:

Adore God's awesomeness

Believe in God

Confess to God

Dwell on God's beauty

Express your heart

Find time

Give thanks for all things

Humble yourself

Invite others to join you

Joyfully go to God

Keep a prayer journal

Listen to God

Meditate on God's greatness

Notice the needs of others

Open your heart

Push away distractions

Quietly reflect on God's goodness

Rest in God's wisdom

Submit to God's will

Trust in God's faithfulness

Unceasingly seek God

Visit God's house

Worship God

e**X**perience God's love

Yield to God

Zealously pursue God

As I review this list my kids wrote I am reminded of an old saying: "Where prayer begins, my worries end." Not only is prayer one of the best gifts I can give my kids, it's also the best gift I can give myself.

TODAY'S TOOLS

Prayer

Dear God,

Forgive me for all the times I get so lazy or distracted that I forget to pray.

Remind me to pray for my kids every day, whenever I think of them. Bring to my attention their needs and fears and wishes. Teach me to pray regularly and sincerely and desperately for each one of them.

Give me wisdom and courage and love as I parent my children. Help me to place them in your hands so that you can make them and mold them into adults with godly character.

Guide them.

Encourage them.

Strengthen them.

Bless them.

Protect them.

Fill them with you.

Thank you for listening to my prayers, no matter how short or shallow or selfish. Thank you for being a God who not only hears but also cares enough to answer.

Amen.

Passage

Pray in the Spirit on all occasions.
Ephesians 6:18

Practice

① Ask your spouse and each one of your children how you could pray more effectively for their needs. Ask them to give you a weekly update of things for which you can pray.

② Find a quiet place where you can pray that you will be a better parent. Pray for your attitude, your frustrations, your stress, your patience, and anything that might block you from being the type of parent you wish to be.

③ Set aside at least ten minutes each day to pray for your children. Among other things, be sure to pray for their health, safety, choices, temptations, contentment, faith, friends, character, future mate, and legacy.

④ Get your family together and create your own "ABC's of prayer," writing down some aspect of prayer for each letter of the alphabet. Make sure everybody is involved.

RULE ⓳
CREATE TRADITIONS

EVERY FAMILY NEEDS TRADITIONS.

"I'm ready," said eight-year-old Dusty as he sat before the Christmas tree with its lights glowing in an otherwise dark room.

"Ready for what?" I asked.

"Ready for our singing tradition," he said impatiently.

"I'm not sure what you are talking about."

"Don't you remember how last year we all sat around the tree and you asked each of us what our favorite Christmas song was? Then we sang it. That's our singing tradition."

"But Dusty, that was the first time we did that."

"So that was the beginning of our tradition," Dusty explained. "I think it is a good tradition."

Within moments he had gathered us all around our tree, and we sang each person's favorite Christmas song. "Now doesn't that feel like Christmas?" Dusty asked, with a contented smile.

Family traditions come in every size and shape. Some are fancy; some are simple. Some require money; some are free. Yet every tradition, no matter how big or small, makes a powerful impact. Our family has hundreds of traditions. These build memories that I hope will make my children smile.

- Every New Year's Day we put together a jigsaw puzzle.

- Every Valentine's Day we take the kids out to a nice restaurant.

- Every spring Tami fills our kitchen with daffodils.

- Every summer we take a family vacation.

- Every fall we go to the beach.

- Every snow day Tami fixes hot chocolate.

- Every Christmas morning Tami's mother bakes her special Danish pastry.

These are just a few of the traditions my children love.

Kids like patterns. In a world that sometimes feels chaotic and out of control, traditions provide a sense of order and security. They give us something to hold on to. They provide a feeling of safety and confidence. When children are faced with stress or trauma, they cling frantically to the familiar. They want to know what to expect. Every child, stressed or not, is drawn to the predictable. This is where they can relax and feel safe—a wonderful comfort zone.

Traditions are like the seams that hold our clothing together. You can't always see them, but without them you'd have trouble. They are also like that favorite family recipe that everybody enjoys and tries to get Mom to cook again. Traditions are all those activities and events that make your family unique. There are traditions for special occasions and holidays, but there are also everyday traditions.

When Brittany was little, she wanted me to read to her every night before she went to bed. I loved to snuggle up with her and read, but there was one small problem: She wanted me to read only two books. So I read them over and over and over again until they drove me crazy. When Brittany was in preschool, she liked to relax and watch her favorite Disney video, and she had every line and song memorized. I tried to talk her into watching something else—anything else. But children love the stability that comes from repetition, so I usually sat down with Brittany and watched it one more time.

Traditions are crucial in every family. A lack of tradition leads to disconnection. Negative traditions lead to anger, fear, or regret. Yet positive traditions lead to a great family.

TO CELEBRATE

Family traditions seem to naturally attach themselves to special occasions. These are great excuses to celebrate and do something memorable. Celebrations are powerful ways of honoring people and events. Every family needs more celebrations and creative ways to make these celebrations memorable. Your ability to celebrate is limited only by your imagination.

We have fun traditions in our family to celebrate:

① anniversaries
② birthdays and half-birthdays
③ the first and last days of school
④ Mother's Day and Father's Day
⑤ the entire Christmas season
⑥ New Year's Eve and Day

⑦ Valentine's Day
⑧ Easter morning
⑨ Memorial Day
⑩ Independence Day
⑪ Labor Day
⑫ Thanksgiving

Each of these days has some special and unique tradition associated with it. Watching the movie *The Patriot* for Independence Day (when our kids were old enough), driving aimlessly for hours to look at the lights during the Christmas season, and enjoying baskets overflowing with goodies for Easter. These are absolutely wonderful, but I want even more traditions. I think we should celebrate Presidents' Day, Veterans Day, Palm Sunday, Passover, Cinco de Mayo, and the first day of summer. I know a family who comes up with weird facts about past presidents for Presidents' Day and stays up all night for the first day of summer.

Everybody loves to celebrate. When I was a child, my family would celebrate good grades with a trip to a fancy restaurant. We'd dress up and have a great time. We also celebrated things such as a new home or a new car. There are thousands of excuses for a good celebration:

- a completed project

- good behavior

- an answer to prayer

- someone coming home from a trip

- accomplishments of any kind

Make a tradition that might involve cake, ice cream, posters, games, fireworks, music, gifts, dancing, cheering, and laughing. These will all create traditions you will never forget. Your children wish you would celebrate more—I guarantee it.

TO REMEMBER

Traditions are one of the best ways to make memories. Traditions pull the past into the present and then push it all into the future, where at some unknown time you can retrieve it and smile at the priceless treasure trove of memories. When Tami and I got married, one of our friends gave us a book about building traditions and memories. In the front of the book he wrote, "Memories are some of the most important things we have. Certainly they can be a medicinal balm in troubled times." This friend went on to encourage us to create "meaningful and lasting positive family memories." The principle he shared with us on that day is one I've never forgotten.

My parents gave me some wonderful memories. There were Christmas traditions of putting up the tree with my family and birthday traditions in which Mom would write a letter to each of us on our special day. We also had Easter traditions of getting new clothes, eating a special breakfast, and posing for Dad to take our pictures. There were also weekly traditions, which I remember with great fondness. Friday was popcorn and TV night. Saturday was hamburger night. Sunday we went to church and then went out to dinner at a local all-you-can-eat buffet. These were simple, ordinary traditions, but they gave me a sense of order as I journeyed through the various challenges of childhood.

My brothers and I can sit around for hours and reminisce about our childhood. The positive traditions that I experienced are blended with Tami's traditions, and together we have added new ones in our own family. By blending these traditions, our family gets the benefits of both. Last year I joined my father and his two brothers as they sat around a table and talked of their childhood. The sixty-year-old stories were as fresh as if they'd happened yesterday. Positive family memories make us better people, whether we are eight or eighty. They:

- improve our attitude

- give us joy

- deepen our personality

- strengthen our character

- help us appreciate what we have

- build closer bonds with our family

Yet most traditions don't happen by themselves. We have to intentionally orchestrate them. This might be hard work, but you won't regret it. Years from now, when your children reminisce about their favorite traditions, you will rejoice about every moment you spent making them happen.

TO BRING TOGETHER

Traditions build lifelong bonds that keep your family emotionally connected well into your children's and grandchildren's adulthoods. Traditions become the glue that keeps your family close and helps each member weather the storms that try to pull you apart. At least once a month, we have a game night, a movie night, and a restaurant night. We talk and laugh and have a great time. Every year we try to find a television show that becomes a family show. Periodically we have family meetings, family vacations, and family events. We go together to Brittany's dance team competitions, Dylan's concerts, and Dusty's soccer games. These are fantastic times that help us all enjoy and appreciate each other.

One of the traditions we use in our family to bring us together is the high-low game. After any experience at school, a movie, a concert, a vacation, or a hike, I will ask each of my children two questions: "What was your favorite part?" and "What was your worst part?" We have a great time, and I learn a lot about my kids with the answers to these two questions.

Another tradition we have is a boys' night out and a girls' night out. Tami and Brittany might go out shopping, to dinner, or shopping again. On special occasions they have gone to Seattle, Disneyland, and Hawaii. When they get back we have a great time as a family hearing about all the fun they had. Dylan, Dustin, and I like to hang out by going to the movies, watching a basketball game, or riding bikes. We've also taken longer trips for a waterskiing weekend, an outdoor music festival, and a Washington DC adventure. These traditions allow us to draw together as mother-daughter and father-sons, but they also bring us closer as we buy souvenirs for each other, show pictures, and share our stories.

Some traditions are constant as your children grow. Others need to adapt and change to be age appropriate. What was fun and brought togetherness when your kids were young might not be as appealing to them when they are teenagers. As your kids get older, let them play a larger part in developing new traditions and modifying old ones. Learn to be flexible, and listen to what they want. Several weeks ago we were going to have a family movie night, but nobody liked my choices of classic movies. Finally Brittany said, "There was this movie that we saw when we were little; can't we see that?" So we went to a local video store and found the movie she wanted. This wouldn't have been my choice, but we still had a fun night . . . and it brought us all together as we remembered watching the movie when the kids were younger.

TO BUILD FAITH

Before our children were born, Tami and I began to develop a repertoire of spiritual traditions. Tami and I both had patterns of personal Bible study, devotional reading, prayer, church attendance, compassion ministries, giving, and various other spiritual disciplines long before our children made us a family. Out of those personal traditions, we were able to create long-lasting family faith traditions.

Creating spiritual traditions for your family that have authenticity and meaning is crucial to building a household of faith. Empty or superficial traditions in this area will create an empty and superficial faith in your children. Choose your traditions and live them. As Joshua said, "As for me and my household, we will serve the Lord" (Joshua 24:15). Healthy and consistent patterns will lead to a healthy faith. Here are ten traditions that will help your children's faith grow:

① helping others
② attending church regularly
③ volunteering for Christian ministries

④ praying (at mealtime, bedtime, worry time, anytime)
⑤ talking about God throughout the day
⑥ giving to God's work
⑦ listening to Christian music
⑧ keeping Christ in Christmas and Easter
⑨ thanking God daily
⑩ reading Scripture and Christian literature

Other meaningful traditions might involve Vacation Bible School or a children's program at your church when they are younger. As they reach teenage years, you might give them a purity ring or go on a family mission trip.

Reaching out to others can be a wonderful tradition of taking Jesus' words to "love your neighbor as yourself" (Matthew 22:39) and turning them into action. I know a family who takes hot meals to the elderly. Another family hands out blankets and coats to the homeless when the weather turns cold. Others visit nursing homes, provide child care for single mothers, or adopt a needy family for Christmas. Brittany and I went to Mexico several years ago to pour concrete floors for families who lived on an abandoned garbage dump. Dylan and I recently talked about what our family could do to help those who had lost everything in Hurricane Katrina. Helping others is a tradition that puts feet on our faith. After all, James wrote that real religion is "to look after orphans and widows in their distress" (James 1:27). Reaching out is one of the many ways we can pass on our faith to the next generation.

Traditions come in thousands of different styles and venues. Yet regardless of what they look like or how they sound, traditions stabilize and strengthen your family. Some traditions may have been in your family for generations, while others are fairly recent. This past summer our family began a new tradition, which I hope lasts a long time. We all gathered on our patio shortly before the sun set and lit the wood in our outdoor fireplace. For the next few hours we asked each other questions and told stories. Sitting around our campfire as the darkness grew and the sparks crackled seemed to enhance our communication. As we huddled close Dusty asked, "Dad, can we do this more often?"

I smiled as I watched our family enjoying the time together. Then I put my arm around Dusty and said, "I sure hope so."

TODAY'S TOOLS

Prayer

Dear God,

Fill my life with wonderful traditions that I can pass on to my children. Show me how to be consistent, positive, and creative with building traditions into the fabric of my family.

Inspire me to celebrate with my family as much as possible, with unlimited joy and excitement.

Teach me how to create meaningful memories that my kids will never forget.

Help me to develop the type of traditions that will bring us together and keep us together.

Empower me to establish powerful spiritual patterns that will help my children's faith to grow deep.

Thank you for the traditions I have gained from my childhood that I can pass on to my children. Let me add to these with each passing year, so that no matter how old my children are, they will know that they are deeply loved.

Amen.

Passage

Celebrate the Feast of Tabernacles for seven days after you have gathered the produce of your threshing floor and your winepress. Be joyful at your Feast—you, your sons and daughters. . . . Your joy will be complete. Deuteronomy 16:13-15

Practice

① Write down specific traditions for the following categories:

> *daily*
>
> *weekly*
>
> *monthly*
>
> *birthdays*
>
> *Easter*
>
> *summer*
>
> *Thanksgiving*
>
> *Christmas*

② Discuss with your children what each of their favorite traditions are. Then ask them if there are any new traditions they would like to start.

③ Read through the ten faith traditions listed earlier in this chapter. Circle the ones you already do, star the ones you would like to start, and add any new ones that aren't listed.

RULE ⓴
LET GO

JULIE LOOKED TERRIBLE.

"Are you okay?" I asked with genuine concern when I saw her at the local grocery store.

Her face was pale, her eyes bloodshot, and her mouth drawn tight. She gave me a forlorn look and said, "I can't stop crying."

"What happened?"

"Jordan just left for college, and our house is so empty I can't stand it." Tears began to collect in her eyes, and she tried to discreetly wipe them away.

"Since he's so close, I'm sure he'll be home a lot," I encouraged her.

"I know, but it's not the same," Julie said. "I'm so used to Caleb and me focusing on the kids. Now that they are all gone I don't know what to do." She looked at the floor for a moment and then said with determination, "I don't think I can let go!"

Your ultimate purpose as a parent is to work yourself out of a job. Your goal is to spend some eighteen years preparing your children for the world of adulthood. For their whole lives you have poured yourself into them—loving, encouraging, teaching, protecting, worrying, disciplining, praying, feeding, transporting, and giving. Then somewhere between their eighteenth and twenty-fourth birthdays, you have to let go.

For some parents it's easy, and for some it is hard. Yet either way, it is a powerful milestone that marks the changing of both your life and theirs.

Ever since your children learned to walk, they have been pushing toward independence. Kids battle for freedom. They want to do things their way, according to their timetable. Your job as a parent is to slowly, steadily dole out freedom as they show that they have the maturity to handle it in a responsible way. Over the years you move from a point of total control to a point of letting go. You started as the center of their universe, but as they stretched their wings, things like school, friends, faith, hobbies, dating, and dreams began to take an increasingly significant role. This is normal and healthy and good.

Your kids need you to let go, and they need you to let go in a positive way. To let go too soon can lead to disastrous life choices, but to hold on too long can create an unhealthy dependence or force an angry break. Some healthy reasons to let go are:

- for college
- for marriage
- for a job
- for growth
- for peace
- for consequences

Letting go allows both you and your children to move into the future. To refuse to let go traps you in the past. It doesn't allow you to celebrate the next season of your family's life. Yet some parents find it hard to imagine this next season in a positive way. For them the very thought of it triggers sleepless nights, heartbreaking grief, or countless worries. If letting go is difficult, stop for a moment to ask yourself why. Six common reasons parents struggle are:

① fear
② insecurity
③ need for control
④ need to be needed
⑤ unresolved parent-child issues
⑥ pride

Face your struggles and resolve what needs to be resolved so this next season can be as positive and exciting as possible.

Family life does not need to end when you launch your children. It simply transitions into something different. You will still have opportunities to assist, encourage, and affect them. One of the major differences is that you will have a relationship with them as peers, not as adults to kids. Your children will always be your children, so release them intentionally and joyfully. For most people, the time after their children leave home is actually longer than the time the kids lived at home. It only makes sense to learn to adapt. Here are seven positive ways to let go.

> *With a good relationship.* The teenage years, when your kids push hard for identity, independence, and individuality, can challenge your relationship with them. Their choices during this time may not be the choices you would wish for them.

Yet don't let this block or undermine your relationship. Your children need your love now more than at any other time in their lives. Remember that you don't have to agree on everything to have a good relationship. Forgive them for their foolishness and immaturity while accepting that there will be differences. Keep the communication lines open and show them how much you care every chance you get.

With a plan. When you begin a journey, it's nice to know where you're going and how you plan to get there. Launching your children is much the same, except that parents don't always have as much say and control as they'd like. Some young adults are drawn to plans; others love the freedom of spontaneity. Sit down and listen to their dreams, then if they want, help them chart out a rough plan for the next one to five years. This can be a great help to them. Yet don't push or manipulate them to do things your way. It's their life, and you are only offering assistance. It's their choice as to whether they accept it or not.

With a respect for their adulthood. Few kids are as completely ready to be launched as they think they are. Yet it's something that needs to happen. It's a part of their growth. As a parent, you must respect their space. Too often I have young adults or young couples in my office who are frustrated, sometimes to the point of anger, because they feel as if their parents won't honor their boundaries. They love their families, but there are things they wish to do on their own. Talk to your young adult kids about what you need to do to respect their independence, boundaries, and adulthood.

With a blessing. Certain cultures launch their kids with a blessing. This is an affirmation, an encouragement, or a dream. It is a way of building up your children and stretching them to higher possibilities than they thought possible. It is a means of letting them know that you believe the best in them. A blessing frequently has at least two components. There is the *verbal* aspect, in which your blessing is either thoughtfully spoken or written in such a way that it will be remembered. Then there is the *symbolic* aspect, in which you provide some physical token or gift to give your blessing a concrete dimension. A blessing is a great way to let go.

With a commitment. Your relationship does not end when you let go. You will always be your children's parent, and that carries with it a commitment to love them, pray for them, and believe in them. Well after your formal parenting is completed, your children may still come to you with requests for you to loan money, provide short-term housing, continue family traditions, share wisdom, watch grandchildren, help with projects, be a sympathetic ear, or do a host of other favors. Tami and I both know that our parents are still committed to us in a hundred different ways. This is a great feeling.

With a party. There is nothing so joyful as a good party. Your child's launch into the adult world is cause for celebration. He has passed many milestones in his life, and you have endured many challenges. You both have reasons to celebrate—something is ending and something new is beginning. This is a time of joy and excitement and celebration. If there are tears, let them be tears of gladness. Send him off with laughter and dancing and singing. Bake a cake and invite everybody and anybody who has ever cared or had an impact on your child. Let go with a party.

With a return invitation. My dream for my children is that I will let go so positively that they will want to come back. I want my kids to know that I will always have an open-door policy, whether it's one month or ten years after they've been launched. I want them to know, without a doubt, that they are welcome to return for holidays, family trips, traditions, encouragement, birthdays, wisdom, crisis management, or whatever else they need. I want to be generous with my kids after they've been launched. A return invitation keeps your family connected and reminds both you and your children that caring doesn't have an age limit.

If you can let go in these seven positive ways, you have done a fantastic job. Parenting is not easy, and neither is letting go. Yet launching your children is a necessary step in the cycle of life. To have a great family, you must let go with grace. Erma Bombeck describes the process like this:

I see children as kites. You spend a lifetime trying to get them off the ground. You run with them until you're both breathless. . . . They crash. . . . You add a longer tail. You patch and comfort, adjust and teach—and assure them that someday they will fly. Finally they are airborne, but they need more string, and you keep letting it out. . . . You know it won't be long before that beautiful creature will snap the lifeline that bound you together and soar—free and alone. Only then do you know you did your job.

My only daughter, Brittany, is a beautiful kite who loves to soar. She enjoys time with the family, but she also relishes her time with her friends. She is in her final year of high school, and she frequently tugs on the string that ties her to earth. She is looking at colleges and talks a lot about all she wants to do when she is free. Soon we will let go and watch her dance with the clouds. After she sails into the sky, we will not see her as often, for the clouds will frequently block our view. Yet I know there will be glorious sunny days when she draws close once again. Wherever the winds of life take our children, they will always be our children, and we will always be a family.

TODAY'S TOOLS

Prayer

Dear God,
   Sometimes I don't want to let go of my children. I want to hold them close and never let them go. I worry and fret. Help me to relax and trust you with my children.
   Help me to let go with:
   a peaceful and positive relationship

a trust that there is a solid plan for their future
a respect for them and their adulthood
an encouraging blessing for them to be the best that they can be
a commitment to be a source of love, prayer, and wisdom for them
a celebration of their strengths, achievements, and potential
an invitation to return whenever they need a reminder they're loved
Thank you for my children and my time as a parent. Yet let me never
forget that families last a lifetime.
Amen.

Passage

Then Joshua blessed them and sent them away.
Joshua 22:6

Practice

1. Review with your spouse or a good friend some of your favorite memories of each one of your children.
2. Gather photos, mementos, and written memories of each child. Place these in a scrapbook that you can give them when it is time to let go.
3. Write down a blessing for each of your children that includes recognition of positive deeds, acknowledgment of good character, encouragement for dreams, challenges for future accomplishments, and validation of a great legacy.

WRAPPING UP

I WISH I WERE A BETTER PARENT.

I know the right things to do, at least most of the time. I have a PhD in clinical and counseling psychology, with a specialty in marriage and family therapy. I've read hundreds of books and articles. I've worked with thousands of families over the past twenty-five years. You'd think I'd have this parenting thing down pat, but I don't.

I get angry and frustrated.

I get stressed and impatient.

I say things I wish I didn't say.

I yell and get sarcastic.

My kids say I get grumpy when I'm tired or hungry. They say that sometimes I flip out over stupid or irrelevant things. At certain times they think I'm a control freak and I have to have it my way. I hate these things about myself.

I'm not the perfect parent I always wanted to be, but I try hard.

I have tried all twenty of these rules, and I regularly encourage other parents in each of these. As you reflect back on these rules, consider the following points:

① Applaud the rules you are currently following well.
② Choose one of these rules to work on this week.
③ Reread your favorite rules and discuss each one with your spouse or someone who cares.
④ Don't expect to follow any of the rules perfectly all the time.

As I write these words, I'm flying home from Disneyland with Tami and our kids. We had five great days—laughing, talking, playing, sharing, and having fun. It's late at night, Dylan is on my right side discussing a book he is reading for school, and Dusty is on my left side sleeping with his head on my shoulder. I love my kids, and I hope they love me.

Dusty stirs and starts reading the last few sentences I've just written. He's quiet. Then he blurts out, "Hope? Hope? You wrote *hope*."

"Yes," I say.

"You don't need to hope," he says with a smile. "Of course we do."

I give him a hug as the plane lands in Portland.

"That was a good trip," he says, "but I'm ready to go home."

"So am I, Dusty. So am I."

FOCUS ON THE FAMILY®

Welcome to the family!

Whether you purchased this book, borrowed it, or received it as a gift, we're glad you're reading it. It's just one of the many helpful, encouraging, and biblically based resources produced by Focus on the Family for people in all stages of life.

Focus began in 1977 with the vision of one man, Dr. James Dobson, a licensed psychologist and author of numerous best-selling books on marriage, parenting, and family. Alarmed by the societal, political, and economic pressures that were threatening the existence of the American family, Dr. Dobson founded Focus on the Family with one employee and a once-a-week radio broadcast aired on 36 stations.

Now an international organization reaching millions of people daily, Focus on the Family is dedicated to preserving values and strengthening and encouraging families through the life-changing message of Jesus Christ.

Focus on the Family Magazines

These faith-building, character-developing publications address the interests, issues, concerns, and challenges faced by every member of your family from preschool through the senior years.

ALSO AVAILABLE BY DR. STEVE STEPHENS

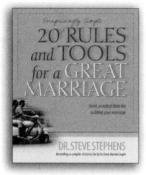

If you want a marriage that's simply great, keep it simple! These twenty clear, to-the-point principles provide practical ways to keep your marriage strong and vibrant. Each chapter includes a prayer for strengthening your marriage and concrete ideas for helping you and your spouse enjoy each other as never before.

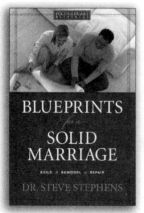

A marriage, like a house, requires time, effort, and regular maintenance. Whether it's light remodeling, minor repairs, or major reconstruction, *Blueprints for a Solid Marriage* offers more than 50 practical projects that help you quickly assess and enhance your relationship and lay the foundation for marital bliss.